5.95

D1598341

REFORM IN LEOPOLD'S CONGO

Used by permission of Historical Pictures Service, Chicago.

REFORM
in Leopold's
CONGO

STANLEY SHALOFF

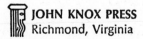
JOHN KNOX PRESS
Richmond, Virginia

BV
3625
C6
S45

Scripture quotations are from the *Revised Standard Version of the Bible*, copyrighted 1946 and 1952.

Library of Congress Catalog Card Number: 77–103464
Standard Book Number: 8042–1499–9
© M. E. Bratcher 1970
Printed in the United States of America

To my mother and father

178738

THE GUILT OF DELAY.

Used by permission of Historical Pictures Service, Chicago.

Preface

My study of evangelism and reform in the Kasai region of the Congo between 1890 and 1921 raised issues so relevant to present concerns that I decided to revise my doctoral thesis for a general audience. At the same time I have tried to retain sufficient documentation for the specialist who wants to verify my findings and pursue the questions I raise. I hope that Africanists interested in the Congo and its history and readers concerned with the life and work of the church will discover much that is germane and exciting in the book.

Many fine people and distinguished scholars generously contributed their time and talents to promote the success of this project. I am particularly indebted to Mr. Walter D. Shepard, the area secretary for Africa of the Board of World Missions of the Presbyterian Church in the United States, for placing no restriction on my use of missionary records. His secretary, Mrs. T. Carl Reeves, also aided me immeasurably by informing me of the whereabouts of retired evangelists or the next of kin of those who had died. Equally helpful was Miss Lizziedine Wade, the librarian, who graciously assisted me to locate stray files and documents.

Deserving of special gratitude are: Mrs. A. L. Edmiston, Mrs. E. Rochester, and Mrs. W. F. Allston, who entrusted me with valuable family papers. I must also give thanks to Mrs. R. F. Cleveland and the Reverends J. W. Allen and A. C. McKinnon, who took time out to write me long letters detailing their experiences in the Congo, and the Reverend G. T. McKee, who chatted with me in person about his service in the Kasai. Nor can I forget the assistance of the Reverend T. K. Morrison, Mrs. L. J. Coppedge, and Mr. Robert Whyte, who granted me the necessary permission to gain access to the letters of W. M. Morrison, Motte Martin, and Robert Whyte included in the papers of E. D. Morel found in the British Library of Political and Economic Science.

    Without the aid and encouragement of Professors Franklin D.
Scott and John Rowe of Northwestern University, I might not have
been able to master the mountain of material that I collected. I
would like also to mention the contribution of Professor Jan Vansina of the University of Wisconsin who first recommended this
topic for study. With his breadth of knowledge in this area, he more
than once saved me from making obvious mistakes. Finally, for his
patience and persistence, I acknowledge my debt to my colleague
at Wisconsin State University, Professor Joseph P. Starr.

                                                    New York, July 1969

░Contents

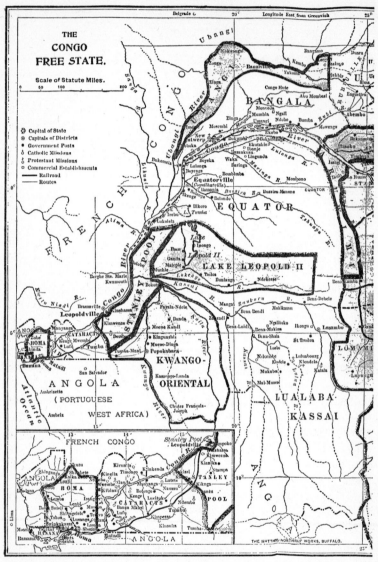

From Samuel P. Verner, *Pioneering in Central Africa*
(Richmond: Presbyterian Committee of Publication, 1903).

Introduction

Although the focus of this work concerns the activities of the American Presbyterian Congo Mission, it is also a study of the region of the Kasai wherein the missionaries worked. For that reason, I have consulted the secular as well as the clerical literature pertaining to the subject. My object was to avoid a strict recital of missionary statistics in favor of an analysis of the impact of the A.P.C.M. upon the people of the area. While not ignoring the evangelical operations of the mission, I have tried to look beyond such considerations in an attempt to comprehend how and why the Presbyterians came into conflict with traditional African leaders, grasping rubber barons, vindictive Free State agents, and hostile Catholic missionaries.

While it is not uncommon for foreign missions to become embroiled in various problems in the areas in which they labored, nevertheless, few missions managed to equal the record of the A.P.C.M. which was simultaneously at loggerheads with King Kot aPe of the Kuba, King Leopold II of the Congo Free State, the directors of the Compagnie du Kasai, and the Catholic evangelists of the Scheutist mission. For the most part, the issues which divided the antagonists were not petty and the participants in those disputes were not insignificant. To a great extent, the difficulties experienced by the mission were linked to the Presbyterians' key role in the struggle to secure an overhaul of the colonial administration.

In all of these struggles looms the figure of William McCutchan Morrison. He was not only an ingenious missionary leader, but as well a skillful propagandist and stalwart reformer. Under his direction, the A.P.C.M. played a critical role in the fight to free the Congo from King Leopold. Although some scholars have commented on certain aspects of his career, his total impact on Kasai history and his contribution to the reform cause has not been fully appreciated. However, while the success of the A.P.C.M. was due in large part to him, two others, William Henry Sheppard and Samuel Norvell Lapsley, were responsible for the initiation of the project.

1

"To Direct Their Attention to Africa"

Anyone interested in the American Presbyterian Congo Mission, particularly if he is not a Christian and not from below the Mason-Dixon line, can but wonder why the segregated Southern Presbyterian Church should have established an integrated mission in Africa in the last decade of the nineteenth century. A question such as that inevitably comes to mind, for it is difficult to escape the memory that the Presbyterian Church in the United States, like all the other white churches in the South, only haltingly and reluctantly approached the black man at home. By every test of logic and reason, it does not seem possible that the Southern Presbyterians could have reconciled their campaign to save black souls in Africa with their unwillingness to concern themselves with the material welfare of the colored population at their doorstep. But the fact of the matter was that no such contradiction presented itself to the men who presided over the destiny of the church. For most of them, the earthly fate of the Negroes in the United States bore no relation to the commandment to spread the gospel of Christ. Their deep evangelical impulse did not discriminate between races and continents, for as biblical literalists they hearkened unto the words of Amos: "Are you not like the Ethiopians to me, O people of Israel?" Once it is understood that the desire to bring the Word of God to the "heathen" had nothing at all to do with the affirmation of the Social Gospel, doubts as to why a segregated church should seek to work among the Africans vanish.

Puzzlement still remains, however, as to the reasons why Afro-Americans were assigned such a prominent role in the project. One can view the decision positively as an indication of the church's desire to avail itself of the talents of its colored believers or one can be somewhat more critical and consider it as an expression of the colonization philosophy embraced by many conservative Presbyterian clergymen prior to the Civil War. Before we can come to some clearer understanding as to whether it was altruism or prejudice or perhaps common sense that determined the racial composition of the missionary force, it will be necessary to know more about the place of the Negro in the Presbyterian Church in the United States and the motives of the sponsors of the mission.

Following the War Between the States, the Southern Presbyterian Church persisted in dealing with its black communicants within a framework of inequality. Those Negroes who remained faithful to the church were restricted to seats in the galleries or compelled to worship at separate services. There was an unwillingness to commingle freely with Negroes in religious ceremonies for fear that such social intercourse would be interpreted as a confession of equality. As was only to be expected, the great majority of freedmen either organized their own congregations or adhered to the Northern persuasions which actively courted them. Thus the largely upper-middle class Presbyterian Church which numbered approximately 14,000 [1] Negro members in 1861 was reduced to 1,300 black worshipers in 1892.[2] It was in an effort to retain as many colored people as possible in the faith without relaxing segregation that the church hierarchs decided in 1874 to establish "a separate, independent, self-sustaining Colored Presbyterian Church, ministered to by colored preachers of approved piety, and such training as shall best suit them for their actual life-work." The hard-core remnant of old family retainers was ultimately incorporated in the Afro-American Presbyterian Church which was organized in 1898 and then disbanded after eighteen lean, unrewarding years. Those few Negroes who still remained tied to the Presbyterian Church in the United States were then attached to the Snedecor Memorial Synod.

In the aftermath of Reconstruction, many political leaders in the South were concerned only with maintaining white supremacy and cared very little about the well-being of the Negro population. What disturbed them the most was the prospect that a small cadre of educated Negroes might seek to rally the black masses in opposition to the existing order of things. If such ambitious men were left free to work their will then it was feared that their brothers would be encouraged to seek black power in Dixie. However, if they could be induced to leave America and resettle in Africa then it was anticipated that the colored rabble would be much easier to manage. Such a solution was reminiscent of the earlier efforts of the American Colonization Society to transport freed bondsmen who might have inspired the slave population to seek liberty.

It is worth noting, in this connection, that as far back as 1818 the General Assembly of the then still united Presbyterian Church had gone on record as favoring the expatriation of emancipated chattels. While the clerics who supported that course were interested in encouraging the exodus of free blacks, they were just as anxious to foster the spread of Christianity to other continents. That is why the Southern Presbyterians were so strongly drawn to Africa in the wake of the emancipation of all the slaves. As evidence of this, the very year that the Civil War came to an end the General Assembly authorized the Executive Committee of Foreign Missions "to direct their attention to Africa as a field of missionary labor . . . with this view, to secure, as soon as practicable, missionaries from among the African race on this continent, who may bear the Gospel of the grace of God to the homes of their ancestors." [3] The project was the inspiration of the Reverend J. Leighton Wilson, who not surprisingly had served as an evangelist in the Cape Palmas settlement of the Maryland Colonization Society before going on to Gabon and then eventually becoming Secretary for Foreign Missions. Once he was in that office, Wilson, who had liberated his wife's slaves on the condition that they emigrate to Liberia, wasted little time in translating his colonization philosophy into reality.

The mission he envisioned was intended in some measure to test the capacity of the American Negro to elevate his brothers in Africa. As a young man in Liberia Wilson had many colleagues who were colored, for it was mistakenly believed that they could labor in Africa with less jeopardy to their health than white men. But aside from their reputed physical advantages, few blacks were thought to have the necessary spiritual grounding to civilize and to Christianize their kinsmen. To remedy that deficiency, the Reverend C. A. Stillman established an institute in Tuscaloosa, Alabama, in 1877, which, among other things, was intended to train Negro pastors. Though Stillman College, as it came to be known, did not win accreditation, it did graduate a number of colored ministers who served the African community and the Presbyterian Church at home and abroad. In fact, it was the black students and white faculty of Tuscaloosa Institute who applied most of the pressure to activate the African evangelical project after the church leaders had approved it. Thus it was an odd lot of colonizers and black preachers and some few people who believed that the services of the Negro faithful could best be utilized in Africa who were responsible for breathing life into the endeavor.

Though conceived of as essentially a Negro enterprise, the mission, nevertheless, was to be directed by a white man. For while Stillman was prepared to allow that educated Southern Negroes could be very useful in the Congo, he was not willing to trust them by themselves since, like most of his contemporaries, he believed that the black man lacked "mental balance, force of character & persistent energy." Moreover, he was particularly wary about appointing single men, for fear that they would debauch the Congolese maidens.[4] Yet the first man called upon to serve was a bachelor, the Reverend William Henry Sheppard.

Sheppard had been born a free man of slave parents in Waynesboro, Virginia, just one month after General Robert E. Lee conceded the defeat of the Confederacy to Ulysses S. Grant at Appomatox Court House. Though he personally never experienced bondage, like all other blacks he suffered the handicaps of his race in the post-bellum South. As a child in Staunton, Virginia, he worked for a time for a local white dentist, Dr. S. H. Henkel. At the age of fifteen, having been taught to read and to write by Mrs. Henkel, he entered Hampton Normal and Industrial Institute. Education, he realized, was one of the keys to the true emancipation of the Afro-American. Most Negroes, unfortunately, either did not have the same opportunity or were not driven by the same fierce determination to cast off the livery of inferiority. After a short stay at Hampton, Sheppard proceeded to Tuscaloosa Institute where he remained for three years. Not long after his graduation, he was ordained a Presbyterian minister. In an area as pockmarked with prejudice as the Jim Crow South, the church represented one of the few avenues of advancement open to a black man. But even colored clerics found it nearly impossible to transcend their own racial community. In Sheppard's case, conviction and not expediency dictated his choice, for his father had set an example of religious devotion for him to emulate as a sexton in a Negro Presbyterian Church.

Sheppard bided his time as a pastor of black churches in Montgomery, Alabama, and Atlanta, Georgia, while waiting for the Mission Board to initiate work in Africa. Because he preferred to labor under the auspices of his own denomination, he declined invitations from the Congo Balolo Mission and the Northern Presbyterians. But when after two years he had still failed to win an appointment, he traveled to Baltimore to make a personal appeal to the white leaders of the church to allow him to bring Christ to "his people" in Africa. Though they assured him that his credentials were most impressive, they nevertheless indicated that the project would remain stillborn until a qualified white volunteer agreed to accompany him as supervisor of the mission. Thus everyone was happy when, in June 1889, Samuel Norvell Lapsley indicated his willingness to join Sheppard in the effort to inaugurate a mission in tropical Africa.

On the surface, at least, the partnership of Lapsley and Sheppard was a strange one. Young Lapsley, who had distinguished himself as a student at the University of Alabama, Union Theological Seminary in Virginia, and McCormick Seminary in Chicago, was descended from a prosperous family of former slaveholders in Anniston, Alabama. His father, far from having worked the fields as a chattel laborer, was the ex-law partner of Senator John Tyler Morgan of Alabama. Though he was young and from a favored environment, Lapsley was not completely divorced from the problems of the less fortunate. It was following a period of urban pastoral work among deprived Negroes that he decided that his calling lay in preaching Christ to the heathen in Africa. As he explained it to his brother, James: "I like the black folks very much." [5] Though they had traveled down different paths, what

Lapsley and Sheppard shared in common was a commitment to evangelical Christianity.

Strangely enough, some of the strongest proponents of the mission were not Presbyterians and cared less about evangelism than they did about white supremacy and commercial profit. Such men as the former Confederate brigadier, Senator Morgan (a Methodist), and Henry Sanford, a Northerner who adopted the attitudes of the South, were predisposed to help the young clerics, for they hoped that the mission would encourage the departure of black people from the United States. Because they were most anxious to promote such an outflow, they were prepared to do everything possible to assure the success of the project. On more than one occasion, Morgan pledged to do his utmost to prepare the Congo as a field for colored "commercial and missionary work." [6] Indeed, he hypocritically proclaimed that "we owe it as a duty to our African population that we should endeavour to secure to them the right to freely return to their Fatherland." [7] It was the only way, he thought, of securing the South in its traditional way of life while introducing black consumers to Africa to develop markets for American goods. More than likely, Morgan hoped that the Negro clergymen dispatched to the field by the Presbyterian Mission Board would act as a magnet to draw the black multitudes after them.[8]

Because he claimed to be disturbed by the maltreatment of the Negroes in the South, Stillman lent his support to the project. In some way, he hoped that the carrying of the gospel to Africa by Negroes would compel the home body of believers to look within themselves and root out prejudice from their hearts.[9] Nevertheless, either because they were disturbed by the likely cost of the enterprise or uninterested in the salvation of Africans or dubious about the prospects of mass resettlement, a number of Presbyterians tried to discourage the effort. Some of the critics raised doubts about the ability of the colored candidates to satisfy the moral, physical, and intellectual requirements necessary to become missionaries. Though he was willing to concede that blacks might experience difficulty in mastering foreign languages, Stillman nevertheless contended that with the aid of white tutors Sheppard "would acquire the fitness to tell the story of the cross." [10] Despite these assurances, a vocal minority continued to express reservations about the undertaking. The opposition was so strong in places as to compel Lapsley to voice his regrets that he and Sheppard could not visit Richmond and St. Louis "as we might thus sooner remove prejudice and indifference which remains in some minds toward our work." [11] Neither of the missionaries, however, was discouraged by the rumblings of displeasure. Sheppard continued anxious to commence work in the continent of his forebears, and Lapsley was eager to follow in the evangelical footsteps of his missionary grandparents.

Months of study and reflection preceded the evangelists' departure for the field. Before initiating their journey, they sought to learn all that they could about their destination by consulting with the representatives of other denominations which already had stations in Africa. Since the rending of American Presbyterianism in 1861, the Southern Church had established missions in such places as Brazil, China, Mexico, and Japan, but not Africa. Advice and encouragement was received from the Northern Presbyterian Mission Board, the New York office of the Congregationalist Church, and Dr. Dowkont's Medical Missionary Institute. A special trip was made to Boston to confer with Dr. Murdock, the Secretary of the American Baptist Missionary Union, which was the first body in the United States to establish a successful mission in the Congo Free State.

Though no final choice of site had been made, the Congo figured prominently in the thinking of church officials because of its central location and the expectation that no barriers would be placed in the way of their work there because of the close contacts of Morgan and Sanford with King Leopold II. Since in their former respective capacities as Majority Leader of the Senate and American Minister to Belgium, Morgan and Sanford had been instrumental in securing Washington's prompt recognition of Leopold's administration of the Congo, they could confidently assure the Presbyterians that they would be warmly welcomed if they decided to commence operations in the Free State. In 1890, it should be noted, most people still believed that Leopold was engaged in a great humanitarian crusade in Africa.

Though their number was small and their funds limited, Lapsley and Sheppard did have the advantage of influential contacts. Judge Lapsley, with the probable assistance of Morgan, was even able to arrange for his son to be received by President Benjamin Harrison. The interview went well as the Chief Executive expressed cordial interest in the project and directed the Secretary of State, James G. Blaine, to provide the missionary with letters of introduction to American diplomats and men of substance in both Brussels and London. Inspired by the President's warm words and encouraged by the prospects of a similar greeting in Belgium, Lapsley and Sheppard set sail for Liverpool on February 26, 1890.

Aboard ship, by a stroke of good luck, the departing Americans met Robert Whyte, the president of Whyte, Ridsdale & Company, one of the leading wholesale and export firms in England. As a prominent Presbyterian layman in London, Whyte was more than willing to help the young missionaries. Indeed, in the years ahead, as commercial and legal representative of the American mission, he proved to be of inestimable aid to the Southern evangelists, particularly when they became embroiled in the struggle for reform. More immediately, when the steamer *Adriatic* docked in Liverpool, Whyte helped Lapsley and Sheppard to get comfortably settled at Harley House in London. With his assistance, they were able to exchange ideas with their English counterparts. Grattan Guinness, with his wealth of experience in the Congo Balolo Mission, was a particularly rich lode to mine.

Once Lapsley and Sheppard had completed their consultations with missionary leaders in England, they wasted little time in crossing the channel to confer with Sanford. In response to Morgan's plea that he use his good offices to help them, Sanford offered assurances that they would not "suffer at the hands of our people [Congo authorities]." [12] As proof of his good intentions, he arranged for Lapsley to be received by King Leopold. Though the day set aside for the interview was a Sunday, Lapsley nevertheless agreed to attend because of the importance of the occasion. Despite the mutual antipathy between Catholics and Calvinists in the South, Lapsley found himself greatly impressed by the Catholic monarch whom he described as a good and great man. This was still at a time when Leopold was able to deceive skeptical diplomats, let alone a politically naïve evangelist. Sanford, more than likely, had broached his resettlement schemes to the monarch, for Leopold thought it necessary to explain "that if American negroes came, they must not remain in a separate colony, distinct from the State, but become citizens of the country and obey its laws." [13] As far as specific advice was concerned, the bearded monarch suggested that Lapsley commence work on a small scale until the tide came in with the completion of the Congo Railroad. Addressing himself to the question of location, "he recommended the Kasai."

With letters of introduction from such prominent figures as General Sanford, Secretary of State James G. Blaine, and Edmund Van Eetvelde, administrateur général des Affaires Étrangères du Congo, in their possession, Lapsley and Sheppard eagerly boarded the steamer *Afrikaan* at Rotterdam for the voyage to Africa.

Following their arrival at Banana Point on May 10, 1890, they began to seek a mission site far enough away from the other evangelical societies to carry on a wholly independent work. According to their instructions, the base which they selected had to be in a healthful location in the highlands not too far from a supply center. If possible, they were "to work among a population large enough to constitute a good mission field and using a language which is widely current." [14] The Lower Congo was ruled out immediately, for it was sufficiently attended to by both the Protestants and Catholics. In large measure, this was due to the inclination of the earliest missionaries to remain near the coast and their inability to move inland with any degree of ease because of the rapids which prevented navigation on the Congo River for 250 miles between Matadi and Stanley Pool.

Before they departed for the interior, to escape the relative clerical congestion of the Lower Congo in search of a virgin territory, the neophyte evangelists conferred with Coquilhat and other government officers at Boma. From there they proceeded to the British Baptist station at Tunduwa so that they might gain the benefit of the experience of an established society. After four fruitful weeks of dialogue and rest (May 22–June 17), they moved on to Palabala, an American Baptist outpost immediately to the north of Matadi. At that point, it became necessary for them to desert the river and to begin the compulsory trek dictated by the cataracts. Brief stops were made along the way at the A.B.M.U. station at Banza Manteke and at the transport depot at Lukunga to secure fresh porters. Finally, in July 1890, Lapsley and Sheppard arrived in Leopoldville which, though an eyesore at that time, was nevertheless a welcome sight to the exhausted missionaries.

Lapsley paused for only eleven days in Leopoldville to regain his strength before traveling to Bolobo to seek the advice of the venerated English evangelist and renowned explorer, the Reverend George Grenfell of the Baptist Missionary Society. On the basis of his voyages throughout the Congo, Grenfell urged his young visitor to concentrate his efforts in the Kasai. As a first step, he suggested that the Presbyterians establish a preliminary base at Mushie, located at the confluence of the Fimi and Kasai rivers. At that moment, he was probably unaware that the A.B.M.U. had already preempted Mushie. He very clearly, however, tried to discourage Lapsley from settling at Kingushi on the Kwango because of the inhospitability of the people of the region and the difficulty of securing supplies. With a determination born of innocence and inexperience, Lapsley nevertheless determined to explore the Kwango. To engage the porters needed for the journey, Sheppard had to retreat 140 miles from Stanley Pool to Lukunga. It was all for naught, in the end, for the carriers deserted when they learned of the proposed destination. None of the Kongo wished to venture too close to the territory of their bitter enemies the Yaka. After some delay, Lapsley finally managed to recruit seventeen hardy souls, and the party was able to set off for Kingushi on December 3.

Since effective government control and safe communication extended only along the waterways, the search for a secure location had to be restricted to sites paralleling the river system. Because it was situated in a swampy region inhabited by the unfriendly Yaka, Kingushi was anything but an ideal spot for a mission. A satisfactory alternative, however, was found at Boleke near the junction of the Kwango and Kasai rivers. Lapsley accordingly mapped out a claim to the area in the event that they could not find a superior place to work elsewhere. By the time the weary evangelists decided to turn back to Leopoldville they had gained a true appreciation of the realities of the Congo. Thanks in large measure to Sheppard's skill with a rifle and his strong constitution, they managed to reach safe haven on February 1, 1891, after an arduous forty-day journey.

Whereas before their exploratory venture, Lapsley had seriously contemplated the establishment of a chain of stations at scattered strategic sites, now he concluded that in the beginning, at least, it made sense to limit their efforts to one good location. After weighing all of the facts: the guidelines set down by the General Assembly, the advice of King Leopold and George Grenfell, and the knowledge gained in their own perambulations, Lapsley chose the Kasai-Sankuru region, his reason being that it was the "centre of influence from which the lines of trade radiate . . . the point of contact, the point of attack, on the people of a vast region." [15] As he saw it, Luebo, in the Kasai, had the advantage of being the meeting ground of five major tribes (Kete, Kuba, Luba, Lulua, and Songye) comprising by his estimate two million people. In comparison to Luebo, Boleke offered access only to small, fragmented tribes speaking mutually unintelligible languages. Equally important, in his eyes, was the absence of any other missionary society in the immediate area. Since that state of affairs could not be expected to last forever, he determined to move as rapidly as possible.

After ten long months of searching and orientation in the Lower Congo, Lapsley and Sheppard climbed aboard the sternwheeler *Florida* on March 17, 1891, for the voyage to Luebo, 900 miles south of Leopoldville and an additional 300 miles from the Atlantic coast where they first had landed. Before they left Leopoldville they wisely contracted with the Société anonyme belge to undertake to ship mission supplies to Luebo. Since the firm had just begun operations at Luebo and was in the process of opening the Kasai to commercial exploitation, it made sense for the missionaries to avail themselves of the company's services.

On April 18, 1891, the *Florida* finally dropped anchor at Luebo, only a short distance beyond the confluence of the Lulua and Luebo rivers. Because of the high altitude (Luebo was located more than 1,400 feet above sea level) and the relatively moderate climate for the Congo (an average daily temperature of about 75 degrees with a humidity reading of about 76 percent), there was less danger of malaria than in the Lower Congo. Sleeping sickness, however, was endemic in some places due to the presence of the tsetse fly. The vegetation of the area consisted primarily of a "deep fringe of rainforest along the banks of streams, and rolling grasslands in between." [16] At the suggestion of the *commissaire de district,* the newcomers decided to locate their station near the north bank of the Lulua, midway between Luebo and the Kete village of Bena Kasenga. In every respect, it was a very modest beginning for what was destined to become a very successful undertaking.

NOTES

1. E. T. Thompson, *The Spirituality of the Church* (Richmond, 1961), p. 33.
2. T. W. Street, *The Story of Southern Presbyterians* (Richmond, 1960), p. 105.
3. John Miller Wells, *Southern Presbyterian Worthies* (Richmond, 1936), p. 70.
4. C. A. Stillman to Dr. M. H. Houston, April 29, 1892, enclosed in the application file of S. N. Lapsley in the archives of the Board of World Missions of the Presbyterian Church in the United States, Nashville. Hereafter cited as M.A.
5. J. W. Lapsley, ed., *Life and Letters of Samuel Norvell Lapsley, 1866–1892* (Richmond, 1893), p. 201, S. N. Lapsley to J. L. Lapsley, November 14, 1891. He was born in Selma, Alabama.
6. P. McStallworth, "The United States and the Congo Question, 1884–1914," unpublished Ph.D. dissertation, Ohio State University, p. 174, as quoted from *African Repository,* LXIII, No. 1 (January 1887), 18.
7. F. Bontinck, *Aux Origines de l'État indépendent du Congo* (Louvain, 1966), p. 192, as quoted from *Compilation of Reports of the Committee on Foreign Relations,* U. S. Senate, 48th Cong., 1st Sess., Vol. VI, 1901, p. 228. In fact, George Washington Williams, a black man, visited the Congo Free State in February 1890 to determine whether it was a suitable place for Negro settlement. He was discouraged, however, by what he observed of the administrative practices of the government.
8. Ultimately, Morgan came to believe that unless the Negroes were repa-

triated: "we and they must . . . deal with their virtual extermination." This was true, he thought, because the white workers would rather die than be degraded by admitting blacks to social, political, or commercial equality. See Morgan to Morel, June 29, 1904, Morel Papers, London School of Economics. Hereafter cited as M.P.

9. Stillman to Houston, in the application file of William M. Morrison, M.A.

10. Stillman to Houston, April 29, 1892, Lapsley file, M.A.

11. Lapsley to Houston, February 7, 1890, Lapsley file, M.A.

12. Lapsley, p. 23. Sanford to Morgan, March 21, 1890.

13. *Ibid.*, p. 44.

14. Ethel Taylor Wharton, *Led in Triumph: Sixty Years of Southern Presbyterian Missions in the Belgian Congo* (Nashville, 1952), pp. 12–13.

15. Lapsley, p. 163.

16. Mary Douglas, "The Environment of the Lele," *Zaire*, IX (October 1955), 804.

2

The Lean Years in the Kasai

When Lapsley and Sheppard arrived, the Kasai was still one of the more isolated and tenuously held of the twelve districts then comprising the Congo Free State. River transport was the only practical way to reach the area, but it was, at best, irregular and unreliable. The Kasai, Sankuru, and Lulua rivers could not be traversed by steamers beyond Djoko Punda (Charlesville), Pania Mutombo, and Luebo respectively. The falls and rapids which prevented further navigation were not the only obstacles to shipping. Equally dangerous were the numerous sandbanks and swift currents which tested the skill of the amateur captains who were obliged to navigate their ill-suited craft in uncharted waters. In the dry season, between May and September, they had to contend with shoals which severely limited the draft of the steamers plying the Kasai and its tributaries. All of these factors understandably delayed the exploration, conquest, and exploitation of the region so that when the missionaries came upon the scene Luebo was still little more than a drowsy trading outpost.

As was to be expected, the early years of the American Presbyterian Congo Mission were harsh and unrewarding. Perhaps the most difficult thing to bear was the absence of any contact with home in the long months between the arrival of steamers. Since there were no more than 950 Europeans in the entire vast expanse of the Congo in 1891, a sense of being alone was hard to avoid anywhere. For that reason, the sighting of a stern-wheeler on the Lulua was sure to bring out a crowd of curious Congolese and anxious Europeans. It certainly was true when Lapsley and Sheppard arrived, for they were greeted by the *commissaire de district* and one of his deputies, two agents of the Société anonyme belge and the lone Portuguese trader in Luebo.

Because of its proximity to Luebo, the evangelists naturally gravitated toward Bena Kasenga which was a village of perhaps

200 huts. For the equivalent of $1.60 in trade goods, nine acres and two dwellings were purchased from the Kete chief of the village. To seal the bargain, a stick was broken, and the chief threw one end over his shoulder while the evengelists did the same with their half. As evidence of their friendship, the Kete aided the BaKongo boys bound over to the missionaries by the state to move the houses to a glade a short distance away. Fences were erected; sheds were built; two cross streets were laid out: Boulevard de Paris and Pennsylvania Avenue. After a while the evangelists moved into wattle and daub homes which they had built for themselves and their employees. The church, which faced south, was simply a large shed without walls decked with an overhanging roof. These tentative quarters proved vulnerable on more than one occasion to the ravages of insect armies and the buffeting of the elements, but they were made to last until the Presbyterians could afford to construct more substantial quarters. With their supply of cowrie shells, beads, cloth, and brass wire, Lapsley and Sheppard bought some goats, sheep, chickens, and parrots. They also planted pineapples, plantains, and bananas. Initially, the evangelists were pleased with the site which was conveniently located within walking distance of the S.A.B. ferry and Bena Kasenga. After a while, however, it became apparent that they were too exposed to the sun's rays, and so they moved to a cooler location on August 28.

On the basis of their limited knowledge and first impressions, the newcomers concluded that the Kete were the people most likely to be converted. Therefore, one of the first things Lapsley did was to study Tshikete. At the same time, Sheppard, or Ngele (the hunter) as he had come to be known, tried to win the Kete's favor by furnishing them with hippopotamus beefsteaks. In the end, neither Lapsley's effort to speak their tongue nor Sheppard's generous food supplements mattered, for the Kete turned a deaf ear toward the gospel. Lapsley concluded that although the Kete had an idea of God and a tradition of close acquaintance with him in the past, they had reached the state where they no longer believed that they needed a savior to whom they should submit.

The Kete, who some authorities have suggested were the true autochthones of the Lulua basin, lived in villages dispersed along the north bank of the river. Most of the approximately 20,000 Kete had fallen prey to the stronger tribes which clustered in the vicinity of Luebo subject to the Kuba. The local Kete were friendly to the evangelists, helpful in commercial transactions, even protective in times of crisis, but not a single one was willing to embrace an alien religion. Their obdurate attitude accounted for many harsh appraisals of their character. One evangelist lamented the fact that the missionaries had been deceived when they imagined that the Kete desired the gospel. To her chagrin, she found that "they like to have the missionary here for about the same reason that they like the trader—we buy their chickens, eggs and goats." [1] Another frustrated cleric complained that they were undependable, unprogressive, and very conservative.[2] If the Kete, however, had been less concerned with commerce and more interested in Christianity, then he probably would have viewed them in a different light, for the Presbyterians tended to judge a people's worth on the basis of their amenability to conversion. In the end, the Kete exasperated not only the Protestants, but the Catholics and the State as well. Though they accepted neither the gospel from the missionaries nor regular employment from the Government, they were always careful to couch their refusals in conciliatory terms so as not to jeopardize their profitable trade relations.

Once they were settled, Lapsley and Sheppard determined to survey the countryside. For four months they toured the Kasai, pausing briefly in each village to convey the meaning of the gospel as best they could and to exchange gifts of brass for cowries and slaves, who would be set free. Everywhere they went they attempted to make friends with the chiefs by promising to send them teachers in the future. For a long time, however, a shortage of staff precluded the honoring of such commitments.

Of all the tribes they encountered, only the Zappo Zap gave the itinerating missionaries any trouble. Led by a chief whose name was the same as that of the tribe, the Zappo Zap were actually a Songye subgroup who had been chased from their original domicile near the source of the Eki River some time in late 1884 or early 1885 by their fellow slave-traders, the Bena Kalebwe and the Basanga. Because they had been forced from their fields, they were particularly hard hit by the famine which ravaged the Kasai in 1886 and 1887. Conditions became so bad that the Zappo Zap were barely able to survive the reverses of nature in their haven along the left bank of the Lubilash. Finally, in April 1887, Zappo Zap appealed to Mukenge Kalamba, chief of the kindred Bena Katau, and Paul le Marinel of the Free State to permit him to resettle his people in the environs of Luluabourg, the administrative center which had been recently established in Kalamba's territory some seventy miles from Luebo.

Though their numbers were not impressive, perhaps no more than 3,000, the Zappo Zap ultimately proved able to supplant the Bena Katau when Kalamba and the Free State came to a violent parting of the ways. As evidence of their adaptability, "they made every effort possible to get full suits of European clothing; to build their houses in imitation of those built by the whites; to use cooking utensils and dishes; to speak French and English; to carry firearms and to take in barter goods." [3] If it served his interest, Zappo Zap, who previously had affected Arab dress and conversed in Swahili, was prepared to cooperate with whichever power was in a position of dominance. Though they never expressed an interest in Christianity, Lapsley, nevertheless, considered them to be the finest people in the district.

One of the most important reasons why the A.P.C.M. was able to take root was that despite their disparate backgrounds, Sheppard and Lapsley complemented each other perfectly. In the rough period of adjustment, Sheppard's physical endurance, practical skills, and ability to converse with the people enabled the evangelists to surmount many obstacles. Equally important to the survival of the mission were Lapsley's business acumen and finesse in dealing with representatives of the State. The enthusiastic duo was eager to succeed and content with what they were doing. Despite repeated sieges of debilitating sickness and the absence of any tangible signs of success, they remained confident. For as Sheppard explained to Dr. Henkel: "I always wanted to live in Africa, I felt that I would be happy, and so I am." [4]

Getting things done was always a problem, for labor was hard to come by and there were no contracting firms to hire as would

have been the case in the United States. Even such a relatively
simple matter as engaging workers to clear the mission site required a trip to Luluabourg on the part of Lapsley. It took him
more than a month before he was able to return with seventeen
men and four women. During the course of his journey, he met
both the district commissioner and a son of Zappo Zap. From the
latter, he purchased two boys and a girl for eighteen yards of blue
cloth and two yards of brass wire. This transaction, like a similar
deal in which he gained custody of a little girl for a dozen red
bandanas, was based on a State law which allowed missionaries to
become guardians of slave children for seven years. Lapsley did
not enter into such arrangements lightly, for he feared that since he
was a bachelor the people would view the little girl as his wife as
soon as she turned seven or eight.

Lapsley had scarcely returned to Luebo when he had to set out
again for the Lower Congo in January 1892 to resolve certain
difficulties that had arisen pertaining to transport. It was only when
he arrived down river that he learned the additional disquieting
news that the Governor-General had rejected his application for a
site on the grounds that the land in question had already been
allocated to someone else. This was a shock, for the *commissaire
de district* had assured him that the land was unclaimed. Since
Government approval was required for the occupation of African
territory, Lapsley proceeded to Boma to confer with the Vice-Governor-General, who was the highest ranking State official actually
in residence in the Congo.

At Luebo, meanwhile, Sheppard anxiously awaited his colleague's return. When a steamer arrived on May 25, he rushed to
the shore, certain that his vigil was at an end. His initial disap-
pointment at not seeing Lapsley soon gave way to shock as he read
the following numbing words of S. C. Gordon of the Underhill
station near Matadi:

> Dear Bro. Sheppard:
>   You will be surprised and grieved to know that your friend
> and comrade, Rev. S. N. Lapsley, while here at the coast was
> taken down with bilious hematuric fever, and the 26th of March
> died.[5]

He succumbed while on his way back to Luebo from Boma after successfully persuading State officials to approve the Presbyterian application for a mission site.

Sheppard, who was to suffer through twenty-two bouts of fever himself during his first tour and later to lose two of his daughters in infancy, was not alone when he received the dolorous news of Lapsley's premature death. Some weeks earlier on April 29, George D. Adamson and his wife had arrived. He was the son of a Scots contractor who had been dissuaded from joining the Church of Scotland mission in East Africa by the outbreak of religious warfare there.[6] Instead he took a job in the Congo refitting the steamer *Pioneer* for the Congo Balolo Mission. When Lapsley first encountered him in Stanley Pool in October 1890, he judged him to be bright and clever. Therefore, he wrote to the Board of World Missions to recommend his appointment, for he was mindful of the church's great difficulty in securing white volunteers. It was when the Adamsons were on their way to Luebo to join the mission that Lapsley last met them at Kinshasa on January 16, 1892.

More than likely, the future course of the American Presbyterian Congo Mission would have been completely different if Lapsley had survived as its guiding spirit. For one thing, relations with the State would not have deteriorated quite as quickly, for Lapsley was a practical person with a great interest in economic and political affairs, which he revealed in his letters to Senator Morgan. Unlike his successors, he was not outraged by the institution of domestic slavery, which he considered mild. Moreover, he seemed to think that the despotism characteristic of the Kuba and Zappo Zap rendered them superior peoples. But most important of all, Lapsley, who spoke French, retained warm memories of King Leopold and was convinced of his good faith. Of course, when Lapsley died the Belgian monarch's reputation was still relatively untarnished, so it is quite possible that the later revelations of oppression and exploitation would have changed his mind. Since he found the "wild African" to be an agreeable person, fresh, charming, eager to give satisfaction, and a keen trader, a man whose soul was worth saving, he certainly would not have wished to see him harried or despoiled.

On one occasion, at least, because Lapsley commented on other than religious matters, Senator Morgan forwarded his letter to President Harrison with an endorsement of his suggestion that the United States play its fair role in the commercial development of the Free State. The Chief Executive concurred that American investment in the Congo basin should be encouraged and advised Morgan to press for the appointment of a consul when appropriations came up for debate. The Alabama legislator actually tried to secure that position for Lapsley, but he was forestalled by Blaine, who had already designated R. Dorsey Mohun to represent American commercial interests in Boma. It is unclear whether Morgan advanced Lapsley's name with his knowledge and if so whether the evangelist anticipated being able to act in the dual capacity of missionary and Government agent, or just in the political role. Whatever the answer, it is clear that he did not exactly have an aversion to secular affairs.

Lapsley's death was a grievous blow, for his ability and character had commended the A.P.C.M. to the State and other missions. With him out of the way, there was now some question in Nashville whether the effort should be continued, for not even Lapsley's presence had been enough to account for one convert to Christ. Perhaps if Sheppard had remained alone, without a white man to aid him, the mission board would have abandoned the project completely. It was in order to forestall such an eventuality that Ernest Stache of the Société anonyme belge contacted the Executive Committee. In urging the retention of Sheppard, Stache emphasized his great popularity "among the BaKuba whose language he alone speaks of all the Europeans." [7] That this should have been so was the height of irony, considering the reservations expressed by some church members concerning the ability of Negroes to achieve fluency in foreign languages. In the end, though reinforcements were as hard to secure as converts, the A.P.C.M. continued to function.

With Lapsley dead and Adamson so new to the area, Sheppard was compelled, at least temporarily, to assume the leadership of the evangelical effort. Acting in response to a resolution already made, he determined to seek the conversion of the Kuba.[8] This made sense, for the Kete had made it clear that they were not interested in Christianity, and the Lulua were preoccupied with their own internal problems. The Kuba, on the other hand, had greatly impressed Sheppard when they came to Bena Kasenga to sell rubber and ivory. Though he could not have fully realized it at that time, this decision shaped the future course of his African career. Over the period of the next two decades, practically every triumph he enjoyed and every setback he experienced was connected in some manner to his commitment to evangelize the Kuba.

The path he chose to tread was not an easy one, as he well knew, for in the previous nine years several administrators and merchants had been rebuffed in their attempts to enter the kingdom despite their proffers of rich gifts. Except for Silva Porto, who had conferred with a late ruler at the market center of Kabao in 1880, and Dr. Ludwig Wolf, who had encountered the reigning monarch at a frontier village in 1884 before he came to power, no European had managed to establish meaningful contact with the Kuba. Certainly no one had ever reached the capital of the confederation as Sheppard intended doing. One reason for that was the threat of the *Nyimi* (king) to decapitate anyone who helped strangers to penetrate the state by parting the Raffia Curtain which shrouded the kingdom. Despite the handicap of not knowing the exact location of his destination and the recognition that his race was not a passport, Sheppard was determined to assay the difficult journey. Somehow he believed that the purity of his motives would enable him to prevail where others before him had failed. If he had any advantage over his unsuccessful predecessors, it was his ability to communicate in the language of the people.

Accompanied by nine African volunteers from Luebo, Sheppard initiated his pilgrimage the day after he learned of Lapsley's death, by surreptitiously following a party of itinerant Kuba traders as far as the village of Bena Mafe. Though he received no overt assistance from the local citizenry, he was permitted to dispatch one of his men to the next market to purchase eggs. In such a manner, he was able to edge deeper and deeper into the kingdom. For one period of twenty-nine days, however, he was stranded in the village of M'boma until he apprehended a company of ivory merchants on their way to the capital. By remaining a discreet distance behind them, as one of his men marked their trail, he managed to cover considerable ground until he was detained by Chief Kueta of Pish aBieeng. At the same time Kueta was frantically trying to persuade Sheppard to turn back, the merchants he had shadowed were dutifully informing their monarch of his approach. The *Lukenga* (king) was so incensed by his unauthorized intrusion that he ordered his son to bring the interlopers and those who had helped them in any way to the capital for execution.

But when Toen-zaide encountered Sheppard, he was so perplexed by the fluency with which he spoke the Kuba language in trying to clear the villagers of any complicity in his endeavor and his apparent success in finding the proper path without the aid of a guide, that he determined to return home to seek the counsel of his father and the tribal elders (*kolomo*). When he reappeared in Pish aBieeng three days later, he paid homage to Sheppard as Bope Mekabe, his father's predecessor on the throne.[9]

As much as he might protest that he was not of royal birth, Sheppard could not shake the people's belief in the transmigration of spirits. The elders assured him that despite what he claimed they knew for a fact that he had returned from the far land to which he had passed upon his death. Since he was viewed as a man of stature in the tribe, he was escorted to an impressive residence furnished with woven mats, carved wooden bedstands, ivory encrusted chairs, beautiful quilted coverings, and clothes racks. Four days later, the monarch's sons, Toen-zaide and M'funtu, led him to the heart of the capital where he witnessed the arrival of the king in his royal hammock. To the accompaniment of music, his bearers gently lowered him within a half-ring lined with leopard skins and blankets extending for about 100 yards in an open square. As Sheppard described him, Kot aMbweeky, who appeared to be between 70 and 75 years old, wore a blue savalese cloth trimmed with beads and cowries, a blue and white beaded crown with a white tassel in it, and small brass rings, the sign of royalty, around his neck and legs. In many ways, the monarch, who Sheppard believed had 700 wives, was a God on earth to his subjects, who prostrated themselves before him, sneezing when he sneezed, coughing when he coughed, and clapping in unison after his every sentence.

In one of the few times they were to meet, the Kuba sovereign greeted Sheppard as a relative and presented him with a knife which had been in the possession of the Kuba royal family for seven generations. In addition, he sent him five goats, fifty chickens, five pieces of excellent cloth, and a parrot. Furthermore, he agreed to Sheppard's preaching to the people as long as he did not try to leave without permission. Much to his dismay, however, Sheppard found that even though he was accepted by the Kuba as one of them, he was still not able to win a single convert during his four months stay in Mushenge. The Kuba politely listened to his tales of a "Great King" even more powerful than their *Lukenga,* but they remained unmoved. To a man they were convinced of the superiority of their own beliefs and unwilling to embrace others.

When he was not busy attempting to proselytize the people, Sheppard carefully observed Kuba society as he walked about the well-kept capital, which was located on a plateau. Happily for historians, he faithfully recorded the substance of what he saw during his stay in the court. Though he was not a trained researcher and did not always ask the right questions and clearly revealed many prejudices in favor of his own society, the weight of what he wrote in such works as the autobiographical *Presbyterian Pioneers in the Congo* and in several articles including those which appeared in the *Southern Workman* and the *Missionary Review of the World* was essentially accurate and certainly sympathetic.

Like many others, however, he fell into the error of believing that the manifest superiority of the Kuba was due to past contacts with Egypt. In a similar vein, Dr. Conway Taliaferro Wharton, who joined the A.P.C.M. at a later date, concluded that the beetle or scarab design in their carvings, the countenance of their wooden figurines, and the rude elements of Semitic religion in their mythology were all pale reflections of Egyptian civilization. Of all the Presbyterian clerics, the one who came closest to the truth was Samuel Phillips Verner, who maintained that "here was a royal court with fixed ceremonials; a throne; a distinct system of etiquette; a people nevertheless blessed with laws, and lawyers; with arms, and armies; with arts and industries" which had developed without any presumptive contact with higher civilization.[10]

Most of the confusion about the origin of the Kuba stemmed from the fact that the kingdom was in reality a confederation of eighteen tribes. What had happened was that, over the course of three centuries, the dominant Bushongo had subjugated a number of diverse peoples and had established their chief as the ruler of the state. Some of the tribes were fully incorporated while others were just relegated to a tributary status. It was the disparate origins of the many peoples that perplexed observers. Jan Vansina, whose work is definitive in this area, has determined that the central tribes were primarily of western origin, probably from Mayumbe on the Atlantic. It is his view that the culture of the Kuba is based on that of several related peoples of the Lower Kwango with a significant admixture of Mongo, Luba, Lulua, and Pende elements.

Probably the most important and yet the simplest reason why the Kuba rejected Christianity was that they felt they possessed a perfectly satisfactory religion of their own which explained the nature of birth, death, and life in a manner which they considered eminently sensible. The tendency of some evangelists to view Kuba beliefs as little more than mere superstition and heathenism contributed to their failure. In reality, the Kuba believed in an omniscient, divine creator (Chembe) who continued to control the events of nature, but whose acts were not always comprehensible to man. He was thought to influence indirectly such matters as the fertility of Kuba women and success in the hunt, but only if he was implored to do so by man. However, if he was belittled or the proper ceremonies were ignored, he was capable of visiting calamities upon those responsible. Though the Kuba did not have an ancestor cult, they did believe in metempsychosis, the power of sorcery, the efficacy of charms, and the spirits of nature.[11] The Kuba were definitely conservative in the sense that they preferred indigenous values to alien conceptions. Perhaps they resisted Western influences because of their innate feeling of superiority. No matter what the evangelists told them about the sin of Adam, they felt no need to be saved. In no way was their response unusual, for a people are generally reluctant to give up the comfort of their own cult for new and foreign dogmas. Even the Japanese, who were so anxious to emulate the West in the late nineteenth century, resisted the introduction of Christianity. Since the Kuba, like the Chinese, tried to preserve every aspect of their unique society from corruption and change, they paid a heavy price for their resistance in the end.

If Kot aMbweeky had eagerly received Sheppard, he was not as willing to see him go. In fact, the evangelist was only allowed to depart after he had agreed to leave two of his bearers behind as a guarantee of his pledge to return in one year as calculated by the tying of a knot at the appearance of each new moon. Whatever the monarch's motive for seeking to discourage his exit, Sheppard was justified in anticipating success when he came back, for the Kuba sovereign had promised to provide him with nine acres and two houses as the nucleus of a Presbyterian station in the capital. When he left, Sheppard had no idea that because of his association with the reigning monarch and his sons he would be viewed as an enemy by all succeeding Kuba overlords. At that point, all that he was thinking about was going home and getting married. So not long after his return from Mushenge he set sail for the United States in July 1893. Though he was greatly pleased by the honors that came his way, particularly his election as a fellow of the Royal Geographical Society, nothing was as important to him as his wedding to Lucy Gantt, a Birmingham schoolteacher whom he had met while he was at Tuscaloosa.

With both Lapsley and Sheppard gone, the A.P.C.M. almost lost its identity. Conditions became so bad that the Catholics even took pity on Adamson, who experienced considerable difficulty in trying to manage the mission's affairs. Père Constant De Deken reported that the "poor man" was living in the most pitiable manner.[12] When Mohun conferred with Adamson at Luebo on December 28, 1893, during the course of an inspection tour, he roughly chided him for having drawn a check against his (Mohun's) account in Boma. Far from sympathizing with him when he pleaded for aid in dealing with the Government, Mohun recorded his opinion that he was "an ignorant fool of a Scotchman" who deserved to be dressed down for his incompetence.[13]

In Adamson's defense, it should be recognized that it was not possible for one man or even a few to conduct a successful missionary effort in the Kasai without assistance. Indeed, if it had not been for the arrival of the Reverends Arthur Rowbotham and DeWitt Clinton Snyder and their wives on May 24, 1893, Sheppard might not have found a viable mission to return to. Though both men were appointed from the St. John's Presbytery in Florida, neither was born in the South. Whereas Snyder was a pharmacist from Brooklyn who was a descendant of the celebrated New York governor of the same name, Rowbotham came from Scotland and had been educated in England and Belgium. Snyder was engaged as the next best thing to a doctor, while Rowbotham was expected to handle whatever negotiations might be necessary with the State. As responsibilities were assigned: Snyder attended to drugs and healing, Adamson ran the mission store, and Rowbotham superintended the local work force.

There can be no question but that Snyder's knowledge of medicine was a valuable aid in winning the confidence of the people. A providential cure of a prominent chief usually worked wonders in vitiating the opposition of unsympathetic tribal shamans, if only because it confirmed the people's belief that the European possessed a superior *buanga* (force). Though they might not have been prepared initially to forsake their old beliefs, a number of Africans adhered to the evangelists in an effort to fathom the secret of their power. However, by the time the first doctor came to the field in 1906,[14] the Congolese had come to lose some of their awe of the pale strangers.

Just when it appeared that a foothold was finally being established, the fortunes of the A.P.C.M. suddenly plummeted. The Rowbothams were forced home by illness on September 29, 1893; then Mrs. Adamson died five months later, and rather than remain alone Mr. Adamson bade farewell to the Congo on September 28, 1894. Mrs. Snyder survived then only to succumb on May 27, 1896. At that point, the future of the mission was placed in serious jeopardy, for the Executive Committee found it very difficult to recruit reinforcements for a field where Americans apparently could not survive. Not only was the African mission the most expensive [15] and unproductive the church had to support, but it was the least attractive as well. Most white ministers who were drawn to an evangelical calling preferred to serve elsewhere. "To the people of the Southern States there [appeared to] be no romance in a mission to Africa." [16] Though he hoped that he was wrong, Snyder wondered whether there was "a prejudice against Africa in the heart of our home people?" "Surely brethren," he despaired, "these things ought not so to be." [17] Apparently such was the case, for some years later Egbert Smith admitted that the problem was not a lack of funds: "I can raise the money to send out the missionaries, but we all have the greatest difficulty in getting the missionaries." [18] When he had been confronted with the same problem in 1889, Stillman had contemplated a joint mission with the Northern Presbyterians, which would have had the additional advantage of helping to seal the breach between the divorced bodies. Nothing, however, came of that plan.

When Snyder expressed his desire to return home after the death of his wife, Dr. Samuel H. Chester, who had become Executive Secretary of the Board of World Missions in October 1893, appealed for volunteers. He informed his fellow clerics that "on account of relations with the State, and for other reasons, it is absolutely necessary that we have one white man, and very desirable that we have at least two." [19] While the Mission Board waited for a white minister to present himself for the African work, the basic policy of reinforcing "the mission chiefly with colored men" remained the same. More of them, Chester noted, "are offering than we are able to send, but at present no white man is offering for the African work." [20]

Some of the black workers had been impressed by Sheppard when he had been home on leave. Because he was fully aware of how grave the manpower shortage was, he had toured the South in a desperate effort to win the support of Southern Negroes for the mission. His limited success in recruiting two Talladega students, Maria Fearing and Lillian Thomas, and one Stillman graduate, the

Reverend H. P. Hawkins, barely enabled the mission to survive in the period when there were few white volunteers. Mrs. Sheppard, who accompanied her husband on his return to Luebo in October 1894, was also a graduate of Talladega, which was run by the American Missionary Association of the Congregationalist Church. But of the new group, Miss Fearing was the most interesting. She had been born a slave on a plantation in Gainesville, Alabama, in 1838. At age thirty-three, she began her schooling at Talladega. After completing the ninth grade, she taught in a rural school. Later she returned to Talladega as an assistant matron in the boarding department. When she volunteered to serve in the Congo, the Mission Board refused to subsidize her, for she was fifty-six years old. So she sold her property in Anniston to Judge Lapsley and paid her own support as a missionary. When she proved her ability as an evangelist while directing the Pantops Home for Girls at Luebo, the church finally agreed to undertake her financing.

Under the most difficult of conditions, the small cadre of dedicated black evangelists at Luebo did their best to sustain the evangelical effort until such time as white clerics arrived in response to Chester's appeal. In the end, his call was heeded by two dissimilar volunteers: the Reverends Samuel Phillips Verner and William McCutchan Morrison. Verner, who was born in Oconee County, South Carolina, on November 14, 1873, was a man of diverse interests, not all of which proved to be compatible with a missionary career. He came from a family which had distinguished itself in the fields of education, politics, and religion. While his father was a six-term member of the South Carolina legislature, his uncle was the Solicitor General of the United States in every administration from Grant through Cleveland. Meanwhile, another of his uncles, the Reverend A. L. Phillips, had succeeded Stillman as the man in charge of Negro education for the Southern Presbyterian Church. Through him, Verner came into contact with Judge Lapsley. Following his graduation from South Carolina College, where he had been a brilliant though overly intense student, he applied to go to the Congo. At first, his uncle was able to persuade him to reconsider this step by reminding him of his youth and inexperience and his mental breakdown after college. However, when he heard Chester's plea, he immediately volunteered his services as an unordained missionary. Within a matter of days thereafter, he was licensed as a minister by the Tuscaloosa Presbytery, under the provision for extraordinary cases, and designated business manager of the A.P.C.M. Inside of four months of his appointment, Verner arrived in Matadi on January 1, 1896, in the company of the Reverend Joseph Phipps, a West Indian who had settled in Scranton, Pennsylvania.

Aside from his religious commitment, Verner was greatly concerned about such things as investment opportunities, ethnographic research, and the opening of a new frontier in Africa. All of these preoccupations tended to lead him into conflict with Morrison, who was his senior by six years. Like Lapsley and Verner, Morrison was an accomplished scholar. Moreover, he was a member of a politically well-connected family in Lexington, Virginia. After graduating from Washington and Lee University, he taught school in Searcy, Arkansas, for six years. Though he had resisted a religious calling for some time, he finally responded and entered the Presbyterian Theological Seminary in Louisville, Kentucky. As soon as he learned of the plight of the A.P.C.M. in the Congo, he promptly volunteered his services, for he wished to see "the sun of righteousness . . . illuminate that benighted land." [21] From the moment he arrived in Luebo on May 7, 1897, together with the Reverend J. S. Crowley, until his death twenty-one years later, Morrison directed the operations of the A.P.C.M. and came to personify it to others.

Since both he and Verner were dynamic, strong-willed, politically astute men with an entirely different set of priorities, it was inevitable that they would clash over what course the mission should follow. In the end, Morrison prevailed and despite objections from some of his colleagues, including Sheppard, he decided to concentrate on the conversion of the Luba and Lulua as the best means of introducing Christianity into the Kasai. He thus advocated the mastering of Tshiluba and the translation of the Scriptures into that language. What he suggested made sense, for the Kete, the Kuba, and the Zappo Zap had all manifested very little

interest in conversion. As it was, when Morrison arrived in the
field, the A.P.C.M. could claim only ninety-three communicants
despite years of hard work and sacrifice. Even that plateau was not
reached easily. Until four children and three adults, part of the
population of orphans and workers who lived within the confines
of the mission, accepted Christ on March 10, 1895, there had been
very little to encourage the belief that a single soul had been saved.
Nothing was really accomplished until the influx of the Luba
Kasayi and the subsequent decision of Morrison to concentrate on
their deliverance.

Of the Luba who settled near Luebo, a number came to escape
the ravages perpetrated by the slavers: Ngongo Lutete, Mpania
Mutombo, and Lumpungu, while others had been brought to the
area earlier as chattels. Since they could not rely upon their superior culture for protection, they turned in desperation to the
Government and missions for help. Many Luba saw in the teach-
ings of the evangelists "a way of emancipation from their age-long
status as a slave people, and readily welcomed the missionaries
throughout the whole territory that they occupy." [22] It just so
happened that the time of one of their major influxes was the most
critical period in the history of the A.P.C.M.

Because they became the nucleus of the Christian churches in
the Kasai, the missionaries praised their character. The Reverend
T. C. Vinson described them as being "docile, industrious and
eager for civilization." [23] But the British explorer Mellville Hilton-
Simpson was less favorably impressed by the grab bag of peoples
he saw inhabiting the large centers of the Kasai. According to him,
they were far below the quality of the true Luba who lived in the
Southeastern Congo.[24] Interestingly enough, when the A.P.C.M.
ultimately positioned a station at Bibanga in the heart of the
Lubilashi River Valley, it enjoyed very little success. Apparently
"the Baluba in their own country [were] somewhat indifferent,
conservative and self satisfied," [25] and unlike the Luba of the
diaspora they were far less interested in conversion.

Not surprisingly, then, just as in the early history of Christianity, a large proportion of the people who came to the mission were
outcasts or aliens. As it turned out, some of the initial converts

proved to be persons who were prepared to attach themselves to anyone to whom they attributed a superior force and intelligence at least until they met someone they judged even stronger and more influential. Because they thought that "literacy and the acquisition of a Christian name [were] the marks of the person who belonged to the present age," another group converted.[26] Then again, there were always some "young men [who] found that through baptism they could flout the old men's privileges." For them, the church represented a short cut to power and influence in a society dominated by age and tradition.[27] It was this group that usually acted as if they were doing the missionaries a favor by exposing themselves to the gospel. These fickle and insincere Christians generally left the church early and were replaced by true believers.

Though it was not true in all of Africa, the Presbyterians quickly discovered that the tribes in the Kasai that were united by paramount chiefs were less likely to sympathetically entertain the gospel than the divided peoples. Thus the Zappo Zap and the Kuba proved to be far less receptive to Christianity than the Luba and Lulua, who were not subject to a single ruler. Although some chiefs tried, none ever succeeded in unifying the Lulua, who were dissident Luba immigrants from the southeast and Katanga, who intermarried with the autochthonous population in the Lulua basin and fragmented into numerous tribal groups known by different names. The person who came closest to managing it was Mukenge Kalamba, a petty Bena Katau chief who claimed sovereignty over the left bank of the Lulua River. He benefited from his willingness to treat with the Europeans and his early contacts with the Cokwe, who provided him with firearms. As a means of welding the several Lulua units into a single conglomerate, he created the *Lubuku* cult which was based on the smoking of hemp. What happened, however, was that the Lulua became even more divided between those who adopted the new faith and those who abstained from the practice. For that reason, Kalamba became dependent on the State for support. In return for being recognized as "Roi des Bashilange" in July 1887, the wily Bena Katau leader went so far as to agree to be baptized with his followers in the Catholic religion.

Not even such a spurious title could help him, however, for he did not enjoy the undivided loyalty of the Lulua. Since he lacked a legitimate basis to demand the support of anyone but the Bena Katau, no amount of modern weapons or State encouragement could enable him to accomplish his objective. Frustrated by his own failure and angry at the new direction of State diplomacy, which emphasized closer ties with the Zappo Zap, Kalamba became increasingly assertive and unreliable. Amity gave way to hostility, for the Free State could not suffer his presence so close to its undermanned post at Luluabourg. Relations deteriorated even further when the Government demanded that Kalamba return the mother of Zappo Zap to her own people after she had come to live with his sister. Finally, when the chief threw pepper into the eyes of Leon Braconnier and had the limbs of Commandant Lienart's interpreter broken, the State picked up the gauntlet in July 1891 and drove him into exile near the Angolan border.

As it turned out, the evangelists benefited from the aftermath of the violence, for the Lulua who did not follow Kalamba into hiding were among the first to be converted to Christianity. It was this Lulua acceptance of the gospel coming on the heels of the Luba migration that guaranteed the success of the A.P.C.M. Ironically, after seven years of want, the A.P.C.M. was in danger of being swamped by too much abundance as the Lulua came "rushing into the Kingdom" faster than the few overworked missionaries really desired. To control the flood, the evangelists decided to accept only those Lulua who gave proof of having planted and harvested a crop. In this way they hoped to exclude the hemp smokers while still leaving room for the Kuba to enter the fold if they so desired.

According to Morrison, the isolation of the mission was one of the main reasons why the Presbyterians managed to "overcome" in the end. As he saw it, because they were separated from the other missions, they had no choice but to improvise solutions for the many problems which beset them. Through a process of trial and error, he asserted, procedures were devised which answered their needs and enabled them to appeal effectively to the people.[28] But before that happened, failure, as we have seen, had threatened the evangelists many times.

NOTES

1. *The Missionary* (February 1896), p. 79. A letter from Mrs. Snyder dated October 18, 1895.

2. Robert Dabney Bedinger, *Triumphs of the Gospel in the Belgian Congo* (Richmond, 1920), p. 36.

3. Samuel Phillips Verner, *Pioneering in Central Africa* (Richmond, 1903), p. 360.

4. W. H. Sheppard to Dr. S. H. Henkel, January 5, 1892, in the archives of the Historical Foundation of the Presbyterian Church in the United States, Montreat, North Carolina, hereafter cited as H.F.

5. Wharton, p. 36.

6. The Church of Scotland Mission in Kenya was established in 1891. In Uganda there was religious conflict between the C.M.S. and the White Fathers.

7. Ernest Stache to the Board of World Missions of the Presbyterian Church in the United States, August 7, 1892, M.A.

8. Kuba was the Luba name for the Bushongo Kingdom, just as *Lukenga* was the Luba name for the Kuba monarch or *Nyimi.*

9. There is some confusion, however, as to whom Sheppard was really taken for. In some accounts, he is referred to as one of the monarch's family, whereas in others it is suggested that he actually may have ruled quite a long time before and not immediately prior to Kot aMbweeky II. The possibility exists also that he was received as the son of the king. Then again, Jan Vansina raises the intriguing possibility that the ruler knew who Sheppard was all along, but wanted to extract whatever information he could about the European presence along his frontiers. It should be noted that the name Bope Mekabe does not appear on the royal genealogy lists of the Kuba.

10. Samuel Phillips Verner, *The Asheville Citizen.* No date appears on the clipping.

11. Jan Vansina, "Les Croyances Religieuses Des Kuba," *Zaire,* XII, No. 7 (1958), 726, and *Le Royaume Kuba* (Tervuren, 1964), pp. 8–9.

12. Constant De Deken, *Deux ans au Congo* (Anvers, 1902), p. 243.

13. R. Dorsey Mohun to the State Department, September 30, 1893, Mohun Papers, 1892–1913, Reel 1, T-294.

14. Dr. L. J. Coppedge was the first physician sent to the field. Later, Drs. Robert D. King and Thomas Stixrud joined the Congo mission as did some nurses. A fifty-six bed hospital named after W. R. McKowan, who donated the funds for its construction, was built between 1914 and 1916.

15. According to the report of the Executive Committee in April 1900, it cost $540 to send an adult from Nashville to Luebo. At that time, the salary for a married evangelist was $600 a year, and half that amount for a single man. However, it was estimated in 1917 that it cost $12,000 to maintain a missionary in the field for one year.

16. Ruth Slade, *English-Speaking Missions in the Congo Independent State, 1878–1908* (Brussels, 1959), p. 230, n. 1.

17. *The Missionary* (October 1900), p. 458. Dr. Snyder's letter was dated June 12, 1900.

18. Egbert Smith to J. W. Allen, December 10, 1919. M. A. Smith became Executive Secretary for Foreign Missions in July 1911.

19. An article found in the scrapbook of Annie Stillman as part of the Verner Papers. It was probably from *The Missionary.*

20. *The Missionary* (September 1895), p. 398.

21. T. C. Vinson, *William McCutchan Morrison: Twenty Years in Central Africa* (Richmond, 1921), p. 15, as quoted from Morrison's diary.

22. William Henry Crane, "Presbyterian Work in the Congo: A Historical Study of the Development of Mission and Church in the Kasai (1891–1959)," unpublished dissertation, Union Theological Seminary, Richmond, 1960, p. 54.

23. Vinson, p. 59.

24. Mellville Hilton-Simpson, *Land and Peoples of the Kasai* (London, 1911), pp. 72–73.

25. A. A. Rochester, "The Story of My Life," MS, p. 13. It is in the possession of Mrs. Edna Rochester in Jamaica, West Indies.

26. Crane, p. 40.

27. Mary Douglas, *The Lele of the Kasai* (London, 1963), p. 267.

28. *Missionary Survey* (June 1916), p. 432.

3

Black and White Together

Though their numbers were never very great,[1] black men and black women played an important role in the early history of the American Presbyterian Congo Mission. They did so, however, as individuals and not as part of any great colonization scheme. Visions of the large-scale resettlement of American Negroes, of the kind entertained by Morgan and Sanford, died with them. As it turned out, a want of finances and of black volunteers with the proper credentials precluded any massive Negro evangelical undertaking in the Congo. Of course, those same factors, a shortage of money and willing candidates, also limited the white membership of the mission. In the Free State itself, little was heard about white supremacy and colonization as both races worked together amicably to bring the Word of God to the Africans.

Most of the Negroes who volunteered for service in the Kasai were selfless, devout Christians who had struggled hard and sacrificed much to gain a decent education. A few were from the West Indies,[2] some were mulattoes,[3] and hardly any, ironically, were Presbyterians. They were strong-willed people without any delusions, who realized that if they truly desired to serve Christ in the Congo then they had no choice but to reach an accommodation with the white leadership of the church. Today most of them would probably be called Uncle Toms, for the way they appeased the white establishment, but conditions in the South in the 1890's were such as to compel Afro-Americans to accept the role assigned to them by the power structure. At no time, however, were they ever officially called upon to assume an inferior posture. Indeed, their lot, as missionaries in Africa, was far superior to anything they might have achieved at home at that time.

Sheppard particularly went out of his way to cultivate warm ties with the Caucasian community. On one occasion, he even wrote to Stonewall Jackson's widow praising the late Confederate general as a friend of the Negro race.[4] In return, the white elite praised and honored him. He was so respected that Chester allowed that "although he is a colored man he is perhaps the most distinguished minister of the Presbyterian Church South." [5] Be that as it may, for most of his career he was effectively excluded from the leadership of the mission.

The colored clerics were proud of their heritage and committed to their calling. Althea Brown Edmiston expressed it best when she said: "My one desire is to spend and be spent in the service of God and my race." [6] Their success or lack thereof as missionaries was not dependent on their color, for the Africans ultimately came to view them as black white men. Indeed, one of the reasons why the people came running to Sheppard in the beginning when they were in trouble was because he dressed like a white man and had social contacts with them. Because they were just as culture-bound as their white colleagues, they hardly differed from them in their attitudes toward the Congolese. In some cases, they may even have been harsher in their appraisals, as when Alonzo Edmiston concluded that "the largest man among them is as simple as a five year old child." [7] It may be that, like the freed slaves who established themselves as an elite in Liberia, the Negro missionaries were anxious to demonstrate their superiority over the Africans by denouncing their "heathen" practices.

Though there was some friction and resentment, race relations in the Kasai were far better than they probably would have been in the United States. According to the Reverend R. D. Bedinger, "the most cordial and harmonious relations exist[ed] between the two races, united in a common cause for the salvation of the lost." [8] That was the reason, he suggested, why the A.P.C.M. succeeded so well. Such cooperation was possible, he maintained, because they were all Southern people brought up together in the same church sharing similar theological traditions. That same set of circumstances at home, however, would have done nothing to bring the races together. But in the Congo, Americans, regardless of their color, had more in common with one another than with the Africans or Belgian Catholics. In an environment alien to all Americans, there were more things that united the missionaries than divided them. Even if leadership were exclusively the prerogative of the white man, the Negroes were pleased by the promise of comparable payment and an equal voice in mission affairs.[9]

At times, the work of the black evangelists was made more difficult by the attitude of members of other missions. For example, on one occasion, a representative of the A.B.M.U. (Hoste) objected to the assignment of Hawkins as transport agent at Lukunga solely because he had experienced some difficulty in the past with a Jamaican and thereby concluded that Negroes had a "detrimental" effect on the Africans. As a result, he urged the A.P.C.M. to appoint a white man to the post. Since the Baptists were instrumental in facilitating the movement of Presbyterian supplies to Luebo, Rowbotham recommended that nothing be done to insult the sensitive cleric. In the end, however, probably because no Caucasian was available for such duty, Hawkins undertook the responsibility. What is more, when he had served his time, he was replaced by Phipps. In this case, then, the A.P.C.M. chose not to indulge the prejudice of an outsider.

No Presbyterian missionary was more outspoken on the subject of race than Samuel Phillips Verner. Because he wanted to make the Congo "a stronghold of Caucasian power" and not a proving ground or homeland for intelligent blacks, he was not in sympathy with many of the aspirations of the mission. As it was obvious to him, as soon as he arrived in Matadi, that the English evangelists and the State authorities shared his view that the Negro was inferior to the white man, he maintained that it was absolutely essential that Caucasians be placed in charge of all of the mission's affairs. It was foolishness, he maintained, to suppose that the black missionary was entitled to the same courtesy as the white man, for it was not true that they were similarly equipped. Without ever having observed any of them at work, he asserted that the colored evangelists lacked executive and business ability and were incapable of learning foreign languages. Because, according to him, they cost more to put in the field than they were worth and their presence alienated other whites, he demanded that the Mission Board change its policy. He recommended, instead, that black workers be required to prove themselves at home before they were sent to the Kasai as probationers. So that there would be no question about their role, he wanted it made perfectly clear to them that they were to occupy subordinate positions. Otherwise, he feared, they would act "uppity" and not keep their place. If it had been within his power, he would not have hesitated to segregate them in their own stations. But while he strongly urged that they be excluded from any leadership role, he "generously" conceded that their strong constitutions and innate mental habits suited them ideally for the meaner positions of teacher and evangelist.[10] At no time, however, was this the policy of the A.P.C.M. Rather it was the personal opinion of one man, who modified his own views after he had spent some time in the Kasai.

As was only to be expected, difficulties were periodically experienced in trying to relate the integrated mission to the segregated church. For instance, such a seemingly innocuous matter as assigning a black man as the correspondent of the Ladies Societies proved to be a very delicate matter. Before Negroes could qualify for such positions, they had to run a gauntlet of opposition at home and satisfy much more stringent standards than any white applicant. Thus when the Reverend A. A. Rochester was proposed for that post, it was asserted, on his behalf, that since he was extraordinary he might just do.[11] Much of the resistance to the appointment of Rochester was in reality due to the feeling that since another colored evangelist had shown himself to be a "comparative failure as a missionary," then all the Negroes were likely to be lacking in some way. If one black man fell down at anything then quite often all the others were adjudged blunderers by association.[12]

One of the strangest things about the American Presbyterian Congo Mission was that whereas it was integrated in the difficult days of *Plessy v. Ferguson,* it was lily-white by the brighter dawn of *Brown v. Topeka.*[13] In part, this was due to the fact that in the wake of the Garveyite, Back to Africa agitation in the United States, the Belgian Government came to view Negro missionaries as potential subversives and troublemakers and consequently made it difficult for them to enter the Congo. Indeed, Mrs. Edmiston was separated from her white companions at Capetown when she was returning to the Kasai and detained for one month because of the South African Government's suspicions of her. The situation became even worse as a result of the turbulence caused by the followers of Simon Kimbangu. He was a convert of the Baptist Missionary Society whose adherents proclaimed him a prophet and in his name incited anti-European sentiments in the Lower Congo.

However, even if there had been no official impediments to bar their way, it is doubtful whether very many colored missionaries would have been dispatched to the Kasai following the First World War. Essentially, this was because the purpose of the mission had changed over the course of the years. No longer was the A.P.C.M. conceived of as a pilot project to test the ability of intelligent, ambitious Negroes to convert their brethren in Africa. Racist sentiments did not dictate the change in emphasis, for if that had been the case the Afro-Americans already in the field would have been summarily removed, which they were not. The combination of official Belgian prejudice against colored clerics and the abandonment of the old resettlement philosophy caused the changing complexion of the mission. In retrospect, the truly significant thing was that the Southern Presbyterian mission had been integrated when racial coexistence was not fashionable and that despite some problems the experiment had been successful. Perhaps it was too successful, as far as some people were concerned, for the black evangelists had given evidence that self-reliance, initiative, and dedication were not peculiarly white traits and that contrary to Verner's assumptions they were quite capable of assuming all of the burdens of a foreign missionary. The lesson, which was lost on some, was that if they were able to succeed abroad then they most certainly were capable of comparable attainments at home, if only they were given the chance.

NOTES

1. William H. Sheppard, 1889–1910
   Lucy Gantt Sheppard, 1894–1910
   Henry P. Hawkins, 1894–1910
   Maria Fearing, 1894–1915
   Joseph E. Phipps, 1895–1908
   Althea Brown, 1902–1937

L. A. DeYampert, 1902–1918
Lillian Thomas, 1894–1918
A. L. Edmiston, 1903–1941
A. A. Rochester, 1906–1939
Annie Kate Taylor, 1906–1914
Edna May Taylor, 1923–1939

2. A. A. Rochester and his second wife, Edna May, were born in Jamaica. Joseph Phipps was also from the West Indies.

3. According to the German ethnographer Leo Frobenius, Edmiston was a mulatto as was his wife Althea Brown. The Hungarian explorer Emil Torday and the British vice-consul, E. W. P. Thurstan, thought Sheppard was one also.

4. W. H. Sheppard to Mary Anna Jackson, January 9, 1906, Sheppard Letters & Miscellany. H. F. Sheppard received autographed picture cards from presidents Theodore Roosevelt and Grover Cleveland, and Mrs. Coolidge thanked him for his expression of sympathy in 1924.

5. S. Chester to Elihu Root, July 7, 1909, Root Papers, Miscellaneous Memoranda and Reports, 1890–1931, Box 207, Library of Congress.

6. R. D. Bedinger, *Althea Brown Edmiston: A Congo Crusader* (Atlanta, 1938), p. 30.

7. Edmiston diary, May 24, 1917, in the possession of Mrs. Edmiston in Selma, Alabama.

8. Bedinger, p. 7. Bedinger served in the Congo from 1911–1930.

9. R. D. Bedinger, "Althea Brown Edmiston," in *Glorious Living,* ed. by S. L. V. Timmons and H. P. Winsborough (Atlanta, 1937), p. 263.

10. S. P. Verner to the Executive Committee of the Board of World Missions, May 1, 1896, pp. 6–9, enclosed in the collection of Verner's papers in the possession of Verner's daughter in Cashiers, North Carolina, and Miami, Florida.

11. George T. McKee to Egbert Smith, January 5, 1915, correspondence file, M.A. McKee agreed with Smith's view as expressed earlier on December 20, 1914.

12. Smith to W. M. Morrison, September 7, 1917, M.A. The other person in question was DeYampert. Smith considered him useful, and Morrison was willing to allow him to return to the field, but he wanted assurances that Mrs. DeYampert, in particular, would dedicate herself to her work. Others in the mission, however, favored their discharge.

13. In *Plessy v. Ferguson* in 1896 the Supreme Court upheld the doctrine of separate but equal education, but in 1954 this decision was reversed by the court in the case of *Brown v. The Board of Education of Topeka.*

4

The Evangelical Frontier

Whether the A.P.C.M. was black or white, integrated or segregated, the primary objective of the mission always remained the salvation of the people's souls and the establishment of a self-governing, self-propagating, and self-supporting indigenous Christian church. Unlike the Catholics, the Presbyterians did not attempt to incorporate their believers into a universal church. Rather they preferred to promote the growth of autonomous African churches. In their effort to translate their goals into reality, the Southern clerics relied very heavily on their converts to spread the faith. Two very good reasons dictated this course of action. The first consideration was the mission's chronic shortage of workers. Despite repeated calls for help, only eighteen new evangelists were assigned to the African field between 1901 and 1912. During that same period, however, three missionaries died and eight retired, leaving the A.P.C.M. even worse off than before because of the substantial increase in the size of the Christian population. Adequate relief was not forthcoming until after Motte Martin addressed the Laymen's Missionary Movement in Chattanooga in February 1912, and succeeded in finally bringing home the plight of the A.P.C.M. to the faithful. Upon hearing him, twenty-eight delegates volunteered for service in the Congo. Of that number, twelve were soon on their way to the Kasai to facilitate the expansion of the mission.

In addition to the thinness of the A.P.C.M.'s ranks, the second factor which decreed a dependence on native evangelists was the State law which prohibited missionaries from settling anyplace longer than fifteen days without official permission. Since it was impossible for the few Americans to be everywhere at once, they began urging their converts to carry the gospel to their home villages. Many of them refused to cooperate at first, for they were preoccupied with their own palavers and preferred not to assume additional burdens. It appeared to the frustrated evangelists that their proselytes were only interested in enjoying the benefits of their conversion while avoiding any of the responsibilities that their faith might place upon them. In an effort to overcome this state of inertia, a prayer band was organized in 1899. Within a short time thereafter, the Reverend Snyder's second wife was able to mobilize twenty ambitious young men in a Christian Endeavour Society and Mrs. Sheppard performed a similar feat in setting up the Women's Missionary Society. With this nucleus of dedicated workers, the A.P.C.M. was able to disseminate Christianity over a wider area.

So as to utilize the limited number of evangelists to the best advantage and eliminate any duplication of effort, each mission station was made responsible for all operations within a specified region. Native evangelists were then assigned to separate districts within that zone. Collectively, they were subject to the authority of the Congolese superintendent of the district who traveled throughout the area. One advantage of the system was that the African workers could reach places that were inaccessible to the missionaries. Moreover, it was possible for them not only to stay in the outlying villages for protracted periods of time, but to communicate the central tenets of Christianity in a way that could be comprehended by the masses. After a slow start, the scale of the work became so great that it became necessary to appoint two missionaries to supervise it in 1906.

Ideally, only men of physical maturity, sound judgment, intelligence, and conviction were eligible for assignment as evangelists. But in the beginning, when such men were not available in sufficient numbers to meet the need, inadequately prepared workers with an imperfect grasp of Christianity had to be drafted to hold strategic locations until better trained people could be sent to relieve them. Frequently, this was done to forestall the rival Catholics from gaining a foothold in an area. Though some unpaid volunteers spread the faith without even being asked to do so, it must be understood that the promise of compensation was a strong incentive for many young men in search of a regular income.[1]

While the system of native evangelism and missionary visitation might not have been perfect, it most definitely exposed large

numbers of people to the gospel who might otherwise never have
been touched by it. At a relatively low cost, it permitted the
understaffed A.P.C.M. to carry Christianity over a considerable
territory. Indeed, even the *S. S. Lapsley,* which was built to transport vitally needed supplies from the Lower Congo to Luebo after
the State purchased the S.A.B. fleet, functioned as a floating
evangelical station bringing the message of God to the residents
along the river banks.[2]

As a rule only married men received appointments as evangelists. This frequently created problems, for many of the wives
refused to join their husbands in the field. They acted this way
because of their reluctance to violate traditional matrilineal residence patterns.[3] In most cases their mothers applied pressures to
compel them not to leave home. The missionaries responded by
warning their converts that they must liberate themselves from
restrictive family ties whenever such relationships interfered with
the practice of their religion. On one occasion, the situation became so serious that an evangelist threatened to leave his wife if
she failed to accompany him to his post.

Because they foreswore customary beliefs, African evangelists
oftentimes were subjected to ridicule and scorn by the unconverted
and unconvinced. In some instances, their lives were even endangered, for the masses tended to hold them accountable whenever
death or illness or any other misfortune followed their arrival in a
village. It was always easy to blame the stranger with new and
disturbing ideas if anything went wrong. Such complications frequently resulted because the great majority of the population
viewed "those who became Christians as giving up their racial
distinction and assuming the customs, manners, etc. of the
foreigners." [4] They were encouraged to think along these lines by
traditional religious leaders and tribal elders who feared that the
evangelists would undermine their authority.

As the Christian population grew, the missionaries sought to
identify intelligent, aspiring converts who could be raised to positions of leadership in churches of their own. Potential candidates,
as a first step, were assigned to neighboring villages to observe the
evangelists conducting daily services. After they had gained some

experience, they were allowed to take over catechumen classes, but
it was incumbent upon them to report their progress once a week
at the regular meeting of evangelists. If their performance was
satisfactory, they were then entrusted with small classes in the
village day school and afforded a weekly allotment of three francs
(60 cents) for food and clothing. If, after several months as
teachers, they still warranted confidence in their skill and commitment, they would be assigned to replace regular evangelists in the
field for a period of at least one year. Their probationary status at
an end, they were promoted to regular evangelists and delegated
with their families to work in specified villages for between one to
two years. Those who showed the most promise and ability could
anticipate being brought back to Luebo for further training and
screening.

It was not until 1907, however, that the first five African elders
and six deacons were elected. Under the general supervision of the
two itinerating missionaries (Sieg and Martin), the elders were
entrusted with the responsibility of promoting the spiritual welfare
of the church by advising and admonishing indigenous believers,
observing novice teachers and evangelists, monitoring catechumen
instruction, and collectively resolving mission palavers. Though the
deacons were primarily concerned with the collection and distribution of church funds, on occasion they handled disciplinary problems and imposed fines. Though they were projected as church
leaders, their independence was severely limited, particularly in the
beginning.

After another decade had gone by, the missionaries began to
consider whether the time had not come for them to honor their
instructions "to found churches; to aid in forming Presbyteries,
when the native churches are prepared for such . . . to train native
preachers; and to do whatever else may be necessary to the promo-
tion of evangelical religion." [5] To that end, a training school had
been established in Luebo in 1913 (later moved to Mutoto) to
prepare men who had indicated their qualifications for the pastor-
ate or lesser positions in the church. In 1916, twenty-five years
after the arrival of Lapsley and Sheppard, three of the first group

of elders were elevated to the ministry. However, one of them, Kachunga, who had accompanied Morrison to the United States in 1903, had to be demoted temporarily to evangelist because of his insubordination following Morrison's death. In consultation with the elders and evangelists, the Congolese pastors were authorized to set up a court, baptize and discipline Christians, and administer the Lord's Supper. A step forward had been taken, but much remained to be done before a truly independent church could begin operating in the Kasai.

Though considerable energy was expended to render the church self-supporting, it was much more difficult of realization than either self-propagation or self-governance. In spite of all their admonitions, the missionaries were unable to persuade the faithful to contribute generously to the maintenance of their church. Some villages, it is true, did agree to subsidize the teachers that they asked for, and the native evangelists promised to tithe their small salaries, but for the most part the Home Board had to go on bearing the lion's share of the financial burden of spreading the gospel. The more perceptive quickly recognized that self-sufficiency was nothing more than a dream, for whereas mission expenditures soared eightfold from $5,000 in 1891 to $40,000 in 1908,[6] donations did not exceed $2,228. The deacons collected that sum from 19,206 people at an average rate of 12 cents a head.[7]

Since most of the flock were barely living at a subsistence level, they were unable to afford any more. Not a few of the converts wondered why it was necessary for them to furnish any funds at all to the missionaries, who were visibly better off than they were. Another group believed itself entitled to compensation just for being willing to listen to the sermons of the evangelists. According to Bedinger, it was necessary to encourage the Christians to seek gainful employment, for only then would they be in a position to contribute their fair share. To some extent, however, that would have been self-defeating, for if the missionaries had surrendered their control of the purse strings, then undoubtedly they would have forfeited much of their influence over the faithful. More than likely, if the evangelists' supply of barter goods had disappeared and salaries ceased to be paid to African church workers, then large numbers of believers would have faded away.

Morrison was strongly of the opinion that the first work of the mission should be in the schools. Education was therefore emphasized as a necessary prelude to conversion. In part, this was due to the heavy emphasis that the Presbyterians placed on the Scriptures. At the Bible Training School, mentioned previously, two levels of instruction were offered. The most promising students were prepared to assume positions as elders and pastors while the less gifted were equipped to become village catechists. By every criterion, it was a minimal education compared to what would have been considered necessary for such positions in the United States.

As was to be expected in mission schools, no distinction was made between secular and religious education. In fact, the object of the schooling was to prepare the students to become useful servants of the church. Unfortunately, the mission's mass education program was frequently little more than an elementary exercise in memorization. The pupils could parrot the phrases that were drummed into them, but they showed little understanding of their meaning. After studying the mission's schools, the Phelps-Stokes commission concluded that "the educational activities have been of a very simple character and not well organized." [8] One reason might have been the fact that the teachers lacked formal training and experience. None of this had any effect on attendance, however, for in 1908 there were 17,484 students registered in day school and 32,075 in Sunday school. [9]

For the first three grades, the pupils studied Bible stories. Then in the fourth year they considered the parables of Christ. Having mastered these, they advanced to a paraphrased translation of Romans and First Corinthians. Sixth-grade students had to demonstrate their ability to read any passage in the two Testaments. Other subjects in the curriculum were: arithmetic, spelling, writing, and hygiene. Initially, instruction was in English and the vernacular, and not in French as it ought to have been, if the students were to benefit fully.

Despite all of their work in the schools, the evangelists con-

tinued to be frustrated in their efforts to communicate the essence
of their faith to the people. It seems that there were just no
indigenous words to convey the meaning of key concepts such as
sin, righteousness, and faith. To overcome this obstacle, local
terms were employed with appended explanations or, if that were
not possible, then a Greek, Hebrew, or French derivative might be
substituted. For example, the A.P.C.M. used the word *satana* to
mean the devil and *muangela* for angel. In teaching the Bible, the
missionaries sometimes forgot that many of the trees, flowers, and
animals that were mentioned were foreign to Africa. Mistakes
often were not discovered for a long time. The Reverend J. W.
Allen admitted, in this connection, that "some of the words that
were quite familiar to those of us who were on the field thirty years
or more ago are now discovered to have connotations that are
quite new to us." [10]

To facilitate the learning process, Morrison completed an excellent Tshiluba (Luba-Lulua) dictionary and grammar in 1906.
Also of great value was his translation of *Lessons from the Whole
Bible* (*Melasona*) which included 150 important passages from
Scripture with intermediate paraphrasing. These and other works
by Morrison were published by the mission's J. Leighton Wilson
Press.[11] Earlier, before the decision had been made to concentrate
on the Luba and Lulua, Snyder had finished an elementary Tshikete primer. In addition, some efforts were undertaken to produce
a Kuba grammar. Althea Brown Edmiston applied herself to this
task but, although she concluded it in 1913 and later revised it in
1923, she was not able to publish it, for want of missionary
financial support, until 1932. Unlike Morrison's comparable
achievement in Tshiluba, Mrs. Edmiston's work was defective in
many respects.

On occasion, the unity of the mission was disrupted because of
the bitter rivalries between members engaged in language work.
The bad blood between the Reverends Alonzo Edmiston and
Hezekiah Washburn was engendered, in part, by the mission's
initial decision to favor Washburn's Kuba grammar project over
Mrs. Edmiston's. With respect to another dispute, the evangelists
decided at their 1916 meeting that: "Inasmuch as Dr. Morrison

has been recognized as the leading authority on the native language
. . . the mission directs Mr. Sieg to employ all of his time in
preaching, teaching, pastoral work, and other routine duties, leaving further translations to go forward as rapidly as it can be done
in the hands of Dr. Morrison." [12] While Sieg agreed to suspend any
further work along these lines, he protested that additional translations were urgently needed even if they were not completely without error. In his own defense, he explained that whatever he had
done was accomplished during furlough time at no cost to the
mission, so he resented the abuse directed at him for intruding in
Morrison's province.

Because the number of applicants exceeded the capacity of the
schools, the A.P.C.M. could afford to be selective in its choice of
pupils. Preference was given to the offspring of chiefs and other
prominent men. These favored "strategic children" were removed
from their tribal environment and housed within the mission compound. Their fathers were obliged to send them to an evangelical
school, for there were no State institutions of learning. Some of the
more perceptive adults who recognized the value of education
resented the mission's concentration on the young. After all, age
was highly respected in African society. But the missionaries realized that the church could only grow with the young. Thus the
mission's primary objective was to transform the youngsters into
powerful advocates of Christianity. Some resisted, but others became apostles of Western civilization. Though they might have
come only for an education, there were those who remained to
become converted.

Because of their responsible role, the Presbyterians were anxious that African church leaders contract only Christian marriages.
That was one of the reasons why the Pantops Home for Girls was
established at Luebo and the Maria Carey Home for Girls at
Ibaanc. For the most part, the inhabitants were young girls ran-
somed from slavery or daughters of African evangelists who were
to be brought up as proper Christians. According to Bedinger, the
orphans housed in the mission compounds were uniquely blessed
for being able to "exchange the foul and loathsome atmosphere of
village life for the pure and uplifting environment of the Mission

Home." [13] The few females so favored were taught the essential domestic skills expected of a woman in Western society. They were clothed, given religious and sanitation training, instructed how to read and write, and informed of the proper attitude concerning courtship and marriage. As was anticipated, many of them wed the native evangelists employed by the mission.

Most of the boys who attended mission schools were not qualified or motivated to enter church service. Thus while the girls received a crash course in home economics, vocational training was emphasized for men. Essentially, the program was intended to qualify students for productive positions in the Congolese economy. In order to make their trainees competitive in the employment market, the A.P.C.M. established the Carson Industrial Institute in 1918. [14] Smithing, weaving, brickmaking, and carpentry were some of the useful skills taught. Since the State and the concessionary concerns tended to give preference to Catholics, the A.P.C.M. was eager to show the Congolese that they would not be disadvantaged by their identification with the Protestants. One way they tried to do that was by providing such a high level of instruction as to enable their graduates to overcome any sort of discriminatory hiring. Dividends were expected from the crafts program, for everyone who was gainfully employed would be able to contribute to the support of the church. At the very least, the alumni were encouraged to place their skills at the disposal of the mission.

Since most of the population was engaged in subsistence farming, the Presbyterians also devoted some effort to improving the agricultural techniques of the Africans. Alonzo Edmiston, who joined the A.P.C.M. in 1904 following his graduation from Stillman Institute, [15] was most closely identified with the gospel of the hoe. He did his best to teach the local farmers the proper selection of seed, crop rotation, and soil preservation. By example, he encouraged the cultivation of lemons, limes, oranges, grapes, mangoes, and pineapples and even suggested the raising of squabs. Most notably, he was able to induce the Kuba and others to market their manioc surpluses. On one point, however, he met absolutely no success. As hard as he might try, he could not persuade the men to relieve their wives of the burden of farm labor. In defense of their position, the men claimed that if they were to "prepare the fields, plant the seeds and weed the plants the fields will produce nothing, but let the women go and just tickle the ground there will be an abundant harvest." [16] Though their motives were not completely disinterested, the Presbyterians did sincerely desire to help their neighbors.

Not everyone who indicated a desire to become a Christian was immediately accepted. Candidates for membership had to attend daily catechumen classes for a minimum of two months and then study theology for two months more. When they completed their lessons, the petitioners were examined by one of the elders. This was necessary, for the native evangelists frequently disseminated a distorted form of Christianity. Those who passed were placed on probationary status. All children under sixteen were automatically rejected unless they demonstrated a sincere interest in education and regularly attended church services. The decisive examination of the applicant's knowledge was conducted either by one of the missionaries or possibly by an African pastor or elder. As part of the test, the life of the applicant was inquired into and questions were asked to determine his understanding of such things as original sin, the fall of man, conditions of salvation, atonement, and the errors of Catholicism. The requirements were purposely made strict in order to weed out those who were motivated by selfish reasons. On the average, most people were held back for at least three years, and many more were rejected than admitted. Thus, of the 14,994 petitioners examined in 1919, only 1,737 were accepted.[17]

The native converts found life difficult in a non-Christian environment. Many were daily insulted, threatened, or what was worse, ignored. For some the pressure was too great and they lapsed. Others compromised by retaining their tribal beliefs for traditional rites. Despite the screening, a few fell away because of moral failings or other character deficiencies. But the number may have been no greater than the proportion of Christian derelicts at home. All too often, also, the people were devoted only to the man who converted them and did not transfer their allegiance to his replacement. For all of these reasons, the annual rate of disciplinary cases varied from between 15 to 25 percent of the church membership.

Anyone assessing the impact of the A.P.C.M. on the population of the Kasai would find it difficult to avoid the conclusion that a number of the evangelists, consciously or otherwise, were motivated by cultural ethnocentrism to condemn practices not necessarily contrary to Christian doctrine. Because they confused Europeanization with Christianization, they often acted like spiritual imperialists engaged in unilateral cultural diffusion.[18] Like many of their counterparts elsewhere, they occasionally fell into the error of viewing "native minds as so many jugs only requiring to be emptied of the stuff which is in them and refilled with the particular form of dogma he [the missionary] is engaged in teaching." [19] Since religion in African society was coextensive with life, there was no way really for the evangelists to avoid undermining traditional institutions and ideals which were the main props of "the social and religious structure of the native population." [20] Some critics of missionaries, particularly anthropologists, have been most vocal in denouncing what they consider their serious disturbance of African society. But in their defense, it should be said that they sincerely believed that the end of salvation justified any changes they might have wrought. Most converts, in any case, were hardly deterred by considerations of psychic shock and cultural dislocation, for they were alienated men seeking an escape from a society in which they were disadvantaged. But it is probably also true that large numbers of people in the mainstream of African life resisted conversion rather than run the risk of being separated from their kinsmen.

Christianity was especially divisive in the African context, for the individual testimony of faith which is required of all converts everywhere and which presents no problem in Western society was incompatible with the collective, clan-based personality of tribal life. For the European, religion is essentially a matter of personal conviction involving a limited area of one's life and not, as in Africa, a communal affair embracing every aspect of one's being. Throughout most of Africa, an individual's welfare was thought to be dependent on the people as a whole maintaining the proper relationship with their gods and spirits through an elaborate system of rituals. Therefore, a catechism which embodied a set of beliefs necessary for personal salvation was an irrelevant and unsatisfactory substitute for traditional religion.[21] Many Africans found it difficult to comprehend the idea of sin in the sense that every individual was stained with the guilt of Adam and could find redemption only through Christ. To make matters more difficult, an African who affirmed his belief in the Savior and thereby cut himself off from his own society was not welcomed into any wider Christian union. A Luba convert might find, for example, that he had become divorced from his fellow Luba without being united with Christians from other tribes.

Though they may have been impressed by some aspects of Kuba culture, as a rule the Presbyterians tended to view the Africans as a child race incapable of creative thought and action. Therefore, they thought they had a mandate to recast African society. Not for one minute did they consider the possibility that Bantu civilization might be "adult, aware of its own brand of wisdom, and moulded by its own philosophy of life." [22] Whereas the Government did not interfere with the people's behavior unless it was in violation of State law, and the Catholics and Moslems tolerated traditional practices where dogma was not involved, the Presbyterians were quite arbitrary in their calls for an end to anything they considered remotely unorthodox. Luebo might have been a far cry from Geneva or even Nashville, but the same kind of sobriety and morality was demanded of all believers and some who did not believe. Inevitably, though, there were differences of opinion concerning what could or could not be permitted. Verner, for one, failed to see how the donning of a loincloth intrinsically elevated anybody. Instead of wasting time trying to put clothes on Christians, he claimed it was far more important to "put the spirit of Christ into the native life, and not to destroy the native life entirely, first, and then expect to have to care for them forever afterwards." [23] Though Verner was hardly the model missionary, he did recognize the danger of setting the Africans adrift between their own "discredited" society and an implanted culture which was not open to them.

After viewing African life through a scriptural prism for several years, the Presbyterians concluded that only bride price and the palaver shed merited being preserved, and bride price was judged acceptable only when absolutely essential to preserve the legal rights of a mother and her children. Fewer qualms were expressed about the palaver shed, for it was of benefit to the A.P.C.M. Because there was no paramount chief at Luebo, the Christians commonly brought their disputes to the missionaries for resolution. At first, the evangelists encouraged this practice, for it gave them added leverage over the people. It was one way of translating the traditional African obedience to tribal authority into loyalty to the missionaries and the indigenous church leaders. Perhaps more important, it provided an opportunity to induce the people to adhere to "the law of God rather than the law of their own customs." [24] Second thoughts were voiced, however, when it became apparent that the volume of cases was so heavy that it compromised the clerical role of the evangelists. In the end, more reliance was placed on the elders to permit the disengagement of the missionaries. This worked well, but occasionally the native judges revealed their vulnerability by their inability to overcome clan and lineage loyalties in making a decision.

High upon the list of things the missionaries found most objectionable in African society were the degraded status of women and the institution of polygamy. Bedinger bitterly denounced the "impure heathen practices of young girls, dulling their minds and consciences to a horrible degree; most corrupt marriage laws; slavery still practiced and legalized under the guise of polygamy . . . the laws of inheritance by which a heathen son may inherit a Christian father's wife, a brother a brother's wife . . . child marriage; and lastly, girls brought for the purpose of bringing in money to their owners through lives of immorality." [25] Because they were unable to set aside their own values, the evangelists inevitably concluded that African women were little more than abused and exploited chattels. Love between a man and woman and between parents and children appeared to the Presbyterians to be lacking in African life except perhaps something akin to the affection of dumb animals for their offspring. To someone who was influenced by Western notions of romance, the lives of Kuba women had "no meaning, no beauty, no charm." [26]

At a time when women in England and the United States were agitating for the vote and equality, African women appeared quite satisfied with their modest lot in society. They seemingly preferred to be the inferior wives of superior males rather than the sole mates of lesser men. In their eyes, this was not equivalent to adultery or concubinage. The matrilineal Kuba, in particular, honored their mothers and wives. Indeed, apart from the king, the tribe was monogamous. Though they could not understand why it was so, the evangelists had to concede that African females did not appear to resent their position and manifested little of the unhappiness that had been expected of them. Still, plural wives were denied baptism after 1905, if they could not show that they had been forced into marriage or that they had not known that polygamy was sinful.

As a matter of course, the evangelists preached the sanctity of holy wedlock. Therefore, anyone who married more than once after his baptism was purged from the church. It was far more difficult, however, to decide what to do with candidates for conversion who had contracted their multiple marriages before becoming imbued with the Christian spirit. Quite often, though their faith was sincere, they were unwilling to cast off their extra wives like surplus baggage. In the early years, perhaps out of expediency, the A.P.C.M. permitted them to enter the church as permanent catechumens, if they agreed not to marry again. Understandably, there were some ministers at home, unfamiliar with all of the nuances of the problem, who opposed such "unholy" compromises. One of them, the Reverend S. S. Laws, went so far as to initiate punitive proceedings against Morrison when he was home on leave for allowing Christians to be polygamists. This action was dropped only to allow Morrison to return to the field in 1906. It was not until twelve years later that polygamists were once and for all declared ineligible for church membership.

The Christian campaign against polygamy represented a serious threat to the communal way of life which it symbolized. This was particularly true because monogamy, which was preached in its place, was a bulwark of individualistic Western society. Christianity was a revolutionary force in Africa influencing the economic, political, and social as well as the spiritual life of the people. In a few instances, through the aegis of missionaries, it even proved to be the opening wedge for European rule. Some Africans who were interested in conversion understandably were discouraged from following through precisely because the foreign religion made so many demands that could not be reconciled with traditional culture. Chiefs, for example, were reluctant to cast off all their women but one, for their prestige and power were partially dependent on the number of mates that they had. One Christian chief who followed the precepts of his faith and retained only one wife was almost immediately ousted by his irate subjects who thought themselves degraded by his action. Instances such as this only demonstrate why most converts were people with nothing to lose. If the Presbyterians had shown themselves to be slightly less culture-bound, then they would have been able to relate to a wider cross section of the inhabitants of the Kasai. This could have been done without any great compromise of the central core of the faith.

Certain practices were considered so harmful, however, that not even a sympathetic attitude would have sufficed to preclude a negative value-judgment. Thus, as much as Sheppard admired Kuba society, he could find nothing positive to say about the poison ordeal. It was not that the Africans were more brutal than anyone else, but that they did not believe that anything happened because of so-called natural causes. As far as they were concerned, a person became ill and died only when another person directed a malignant force against him. The poison ordeal was intended to expose those responsible for such misfortunes. It varied from tribe to tribe and place to place, but the laudable objective was always to identify the individual responsible for the evil. Efforts by the Presbyterians to erradicate the practice usually ended in failure, for the people viewed it as an essential instrument of social control. No matter what the evangelists said, the Africans continued to believe that it was possible for pernicious influences to be consciously or unconsciously transmitted. Because the Congolese thought that the verdict of the ordeal was the judgment of the Divine, Morrison reported how anxious the accused were "to drink the poison to prove their innocence, believing they would vomit it & hence not die." [27] Though the State responded to the pressure of the missionaries and others by outlawing the ordeal in 1924, it still survived in the bush.

The divergent views of justice and punishment entertained by African and Western society was revealed by an incident of organized stealing which occurred in early 1903 at Luebo. Eight mission boys, all but one a Tetela (the tribe of Patrice Lumumba), were found to have been systematically looting the storehouses of the A.P.C.M. and local trading establishments. Instead of using his influence to free them, however, as their wives and relatives fully expected, Morrison disappointed and angered them by his intention of handing them over to the State for trial. Their offer of compensation was rejected by him because he did not consider mere payment to be sufficient to eliminate the stigma of wrongdoing. Of course, the idea of punishing someone by placing him in prison just for the sake of punishment was just as foreign to the Africans as the resort to the ordeal had become for Europeans. In the end, one of the boys tried to perforate his bowels with a pair of scissors and in the confusion another escaped.

In an effort to protect themselves against hostile spirits, many Africans secured fetishes. Though these objects were not worshiped or considered divine, they were thought to be effective in warding off deleterious forces. Because the Presbyterians viewed the fetishes as impediments to conversion, they demanded that they be destroyed. On one occasion, the mission ordered the people of Bulape to turn over all their charms to the evangelists. Surprisingly, it was the younger people from age fifteen to eighteen who resisted the most, for they wished to preserve the heritage of the past and feared a diminution of tribal fecundity. Ultimately, the elders consented to the destruction of the fetishes. But whereas the talismans might be seen smoldering in the vicinity of Bulape and Luebo, elsewhere the populace continued to display them conspicuously for maximum safety.

The austere Presbyterian evangelists tried to censor the lives not only of their own adherents but of everyone else in the Kasai as well. On several occasions, they denounced State officers for living in sin with native mistresses. To the Ten Commandments, they added an eleventh against the consumption of alcohol. They repeatedly urged the people to destroy their stills and cease drinking palm wine. Since the Kuba, for instance, considered the imbibing of that beverage to be a sign of masculinity, they were not disposed to do without it.

What it came down to ultimately was that most Africans were not prepared to live the lives of proper Calvinists in the bush. To begin with, it was hard for them to understand why the evangelists seemed so dedicated to rooting out every element of joy and spontaneity in their way of life. They could not comprehend how things that had been considered perfectly proper before were suddenly wrong in some way. New converts, like Daniel Cisungu, felt burdened by a previously unknown sense of guilt which came upon them when they were not able to abstain from doing the things that they had been told were not right. On one occasion, after he confessed his transgressions and promised not to repeat them, Daniel pleaded for forgiveness. If the A.P.C.M. would only let him go back to work again so that he could make money, he pledged that he would be "a niece [sic] boy." Apparently, neither his English nor his morals improved, for shortly thereafter, he was compelled to admit once again that he had been a very bad boy who lacked strength.[28] Though he was turned out of the church, he was no different than some of the Christian chiefs who remained faithful "not because they want to be saved, but because of love of gain, and for political reasons." [29] Like everywhere else, then, there were those who were truly moved by piety and willing to change over their life-styles, while others were motivated by selfish reasons and refused to make sacrifices.

Quite often, the mission's intrusion in the affairs of neighboring villages was resented by local chiefs. It was not so much Christianity that they feared, but the expanding temporal powers of the missionaries. Their worries were not without foundation, for some of the evangelists not only interpreted State laws for the people but issued regulations of their own as well. At Ibaanc, Edmiston went so far as to decree that henceforth:

1. No Catholics alowed [*sic*] in the village near mission.
2. No making gin in villages.
3. All villages must come into line with chiefs.
4. All strangers must appear at the mission on their arrival in the village.[30]

Conflicting sovereignty claims, not surprisingly, therefore, were at the root of many of the disagreements between the clerics and traditional tribal leaders. In large part this was true because the chiefs could not abide their subjects deferring to any other authority ahead of their own. Moreover, the State also resented the practice of the Presbyterians of holding "court," since it was an undisguised slight to government prestige.

Without doubt, the Presbyterians would not have acted in the way that they did if they had not been of the opinion that everything improved under the benign influence of Christian teaching. To prove their point, they contrasted the contented, intelligent mien of their converts with the assertedly ignorant, debauched look of the "heathens." As distinguished from the pagans, they maintained that their adherents were neat and industrious family men who loved their wives, children, and parents. What they claimed was not a complete exaggeration, for the Phelps-Stokes Fund concluded that "the effect of the mission [A.P.C.M.] on the native people is one of the most notable achievements in the Belgian Congo." [31]

The influence of the missionaries was particularly strong during the first two decades of the A.P.C.M.'s existence, when the white man's power was still a big mystery to the Africans. Some Congolese, then, were prepared to emulate everything that the missionaries did in a vain effort to learn the secret of their superior position. A few moved out of their grass huts into white-clay houses with attached verandas just like the white man's dwellings. Others suddenly started building doors to reach the ground whereas previously they were constructed like windows. But windows, themselves, were excluded, for the Congolese preferred not to facilitate the entrance of malignant forces. Though the vast majority of the population continued to cling to the old ways of doing things, even they were not immune to the impact of the evangelists.

Probably the most visible outer change the Christians underwent was in their dress. Whereas many of them looked ludicrous in their ill-assorted, ill-fitting Western garments, some managed fair imitations of proper Edwardians. African church leaders, in particular, were anxious to don European clothes as symbols of their new status and authority. Not only did the faithful dress distinctively, but they ate differently as well. Besides introducing new crops, the Presbyterians encouraged the violation of old dietary taboos such as the boycott of goat's flesh by Kete women. In like manner, they abbreviated the traditional period of mourning for the dead and promoted the use of wooden coffins instead of mats. Even if they had been of a mind to, not all of the converts could make the adjustment without hesitation. Edmiston had to deal with one fellow who refused to help bury another Christian because his son was too young. He warned him that he would have to forsake his heathen beliefs, if he wished to remain within the church. Obviously clothes and food only dealt with the outer man and were not proof of an inner transformation as well.

In the end, only a comparatively small percentage of the people became Christians, and many of them were the marginal members of African society: the flotsam and jetsam of the Kasai, men without positions, children without parents, women without husbands, slaves in search of freedom, and oldsters without hope. Yet despite all of the stress and strain, an impressive number of converts remained stalwart in their newfound faith. By this criterion alone, the A.P.C.M. must be adjudged a successful mission. It was no mean feat, considering all of the difficulties which were experienced in the beginning. Some of the reasons why the A.P.C.M. survived—able leadership, a wise selection of site, the use of native evangelists, and the migration of the Luba—have already been discussed. But one significant factor has been ignored until now, namely, the active role of the Presbyterians in the struggle to bring about an end to the abuses of the colonial administration.

Nothing was more important in winning the respect and loyalty of the people of the Kasai. Because of its great consequence, this matter will be elaborated upon in considerable detail in the following chapters.

NOTES

1. *Missionary Survey* (February 1917). In 1917, the average salary for an African evangelist was $16 a year and that amount was to be cut 20 percent on the orders of the Executive Committee. On the other hand, an ordinary native worker for the missionary received $2 a month, with the highest paid employee receiving $4 monthly in 1918.

2. On September 21, 1899, Chester signed a contract with William R. Trigg & Company in Richmond to build a steamer for $16,000. The *S. S. Lapsley* reached Luebo in May 1901. It was designed for American and not Congo waters, and so it sank on November 16, 1903, killing 23 Africans and the Reverend H. C. Slaymaker. A new vessel was constructed on the Clyde to replace the first one, which was sold for $5,000. The new *S. S. Lapsley* arrived in Luebo on December 24, 1906. It was a $45,000 stern-wheeler and gave the mission 25 years of service. A ship was necessary, for each evangelist needed approximately 37 loads of barter goods a year. A load was equivalent to 85 pounds.

3. A matrilineal residence pattern would have the husband moving into the family compound of his wife rather than the opposite way around.

4. Morrison diary, February 16, 1899, H.F.

5. Thomas C. Johnson, *History of the Southern Presbyterian Church*, in *The American Church History Series: A History of the Methodist Church, South, the United Presbyterian Church and the Presbyterian Church in the U. S.* (New York, 1900), XI, p. 363. General Assembly instructions of 1877.

6. Slade, p. 232.

7. Bedinger, *Triumphs*, p. 128.

8. Thomas Jesse Jones, *Education in Africa* (New York, 1922), p. 139.

9. Bedinger, *Triumphs*, p. 62.

10. J. W. Allen, "The Varied Avenues of Missionary Effort Which Are Building a Native Church," MS, p. 1, M.A.

11. The money for the press came largely from a Sunday school in Baltimore. The *Kasai Herald* was first published in March 1901.

12. Resolution 5 of the minutes of the annual meeting, January 31, 1916.

13. Bedinger, *Triumphs*, p. 57.

14. Mr. and Mrs. Carson from North Carolina contributed $10,000 to establish the Industrial School. C. R. Stegall was in charge of it. The brickmaking press was the gift of John R. Sampson. A saw mill was purchased from the A.B.M.U. and installed by A. C. McKinnon.

15. Edmiston originally came to the Kasai with S. P. Verner, who was gathering curios and the like for the Louisiana Purchase Exposition of 1904 in St. Louis. When Edmiston learned that Verner had no real intention of founding a mission, as he had promised, he joined the A.P.C.M. at the invitation of his friend L. A. DeYampert.

16. Rochester, MS, p. 17.

17. Bedinger, *Triumphs*, pp. 163–164.

18. Ako Adjei, "Imperialism and Spiritual Freedom an African View," *The American Journal of Sociology*, L (November 1944), 190.

19. Mary H. Kingsley, *Travels in West Africa* (London, 1897), p. 489. The

author quotes her father's observation of Polynesia and applies it to Africa. Miss Kingsley was not a completely disinterested writer.

20. Diedrich Westermann, *Africa and Christianity* (London, 1937), p. 2.

21. J. F. Ade Ajayi, *Christian Missions in Nigeria 1841–1891: The Making of a New Elite* (Evanston, 1965), pp. 2–5.

22. P. Tempels, *Bantu Philosophy*, tr. by C. King (Paris, 1959), p. 80.

23. S. P. Verner, "Women in Africa," *The Missionary* (August 1899), pp. 377–378.

24. H. M. Washburn to Executive Committee, July 4, 1920, M.A.

25. Bedinger, *Triumphs*, pp. 56–57.

26. *Ibid.*, p. 159.

27. Morrison diary, January 4, 1899.

28. Daniel Cisungu to W. M. Morrison, Missionary Correspondence, M.A.

29. E. R. Kellersberger to Executive Secretary, December 17, 1917, M.A.

30. Edmiston diary, January 29, 1917.

31. Jones, p. 280.

5

The Zappo Zap Raid

The American Presbyterian Congo Mission did not deliberately set out to involve itself in political affairs. That would have been a refutation of the principles upon which the Southern Church had been founded. Though individuals like Snyder would have personally preferred "to see the United States the possessor of the Congo Free State," [1] that was not the official position of the mission. Indeed, Chester assured King Leopold "that any interference with the political affairs of the Congo Free State by any of our missionaries would not be tolerated by us, nor thought of by them, their only aim being the work for the spiritual and moral elevation of the African people." [2] There were some early difficulties with respect to taxation, transportation, and station sites, but criticism remained muted, until overt acts of Government oppression occurred in the vicinity of Luebo. Then the evangelists decided to break their silence. As they were the only Protestant missionaries in the Kasai (except for the apolitical Plymouth Brethren), they felt a responsibility to speak out. But even then nothing might have been done, if Verner instead of Morrison had been in charge of the A.P.C.M.

If he had had his way, Verner would have prohibited overt condemnation of official policies and actions, for he was determined to avoid disputes with the State at any price. As an alternative to public complaint, he recommended quiet discussions with the proper authorities. Then, if satisfaction still were not forthcoming, and the situation remained intolerable, he suggested that it would be best for all concerned if the aggrieved party left the scene. Morrison, however, strongly disapproved of Verner's seeming willingness to sacrifice the people's welfare on the altar of good relations with the Government. With some justification, he suspected that Verner's secular pursuits accounted for his reluctance to antagonize the State. More than likely, it was Verner's unwill-

ingness to submerge himself fully in religious affairs that drove a
wedge between the two men.

The question of the obligation of the individual when confronted with proof of wrongdoing is still hotly debated today. One
school of thought considers the observer who does not intervene
when he sees a crime being committed to be as guilty as the
perpetrator. Morrison was an advocate of this point of view. He
believed every individual was morally bound to protest against
illegal actions. Only a coward, he claimed, would shirk his responsibility to his fellowman. Knowing what to do, however, was never
as simple as all that, for the issues were seldom clear-cut. As it
turned out, Morrison was prepared to protest at the slightest
provocation, whereas Verner's lips remained sealed no matter
what had happened.

Probably the clearest indication of the divergent paths Morrison and Verner were disposed to lead the mission in was revealed
by their responses to virtually identical rebuffs from the State re-
garding the expansion of the A.P.C.M. For his part, Verner had
devoted himself to converting the Bashi Bienge, a dissident Kuba
group living in the Wissmann Falls district. To that end, he established a station (Ndombe) on the slope of a hill overlooking the
Lubi River. At about the same time, Sheppard and Morrison were
compelled to set up temporary quarters at Ibaanc, a border village
some 35 miles from Mushenge, when their path to the Kuba
capital was barred by Mishaape II. Unfortunately for the
A.P.C.M., Sheppard's royal benefactor, Kot aMbweeky, had died
before the evangelist was able to initiate work in Mushenge. It was
because his successor, Mishaape, was alike unto the Pharoah who
knew not Joseph, that the Presbyterians had to resign themselves
to the holding action at Ibaanc while they waited for the *Nyimi* to
see the light. From September 1897 to April 1898, Morrison kept
a lonely vigil at Ibaanc praying for a summons that never came.

Both Verner and Morrison, however, did receive unexpected
notices from the *commissaire de Luluabourg* ordering the evacua-
tion of their respective stations.[3] Not surprisingly, whereas Verner
believed that the directive was nothing more than a mistake that
would be set right by higher authority, Morrison was convinced

that it was conclusive proof of the State's subservience to the Pope's wishes. Under the circumstances, Morrison was prepared to apply as much pressure as was necessary to protect the mission's interests. Conversely, Verner sought to accomplish the same end through appeasement. At first, it looked as though Verner's course was the wisest, for the Vice-Governor-General assured him that his application for founding a permanent station at Ndombe would be approved before he returned to the Congo from leave. Similar promises were repeated by those Free State officials with whom Verner conferred in Brussels while he was on his way home. In the end, however, Ibaanc was allowed to reopen on December 1, 1898, while Ndombe remained closed. Nevertheless, Verner's faith in the Government remained unshaken. As for Morrison, he was not reconciled in the slightest by this decision. Moreover, when Verner left the field and the mission in 1899, the hard line of the missionary from Lexington remained unchallenged. Timorous sycophancy was eschewed in favor of bold bluntness.

Much of the friction between the missions and the State was caused by the excesses of the Government's native troops, the *Force Publique*. After an undisciplined rabble had descended upon Ndombe to collect tribute and tarried to despoil the region, even Verner had to concede that the use of the *Force Publique* to gather revenue tended to provoke disorders. Because of repeated incidents of this kind, the evangelists came to view the indigenous State troops as instruments of oppression and exploitation. Through their efforts to protect the Congolese from such depredations, the Presbyterians earned the gratitude of the people.

Still, the American clerics refrained from public criticism of the Free State until after the bloody Zappo Zap assault upon the Pyaang, the tribe which guarded the Eastern flank of the Kuba kingdom. In the wake of that brutal episode, numerous refugees streamed into Ibaanc to seek shelter and to implore Sheppard's aid in stopping the slaughter. Twice he refused, for he was immobilized by fright. As it turned out, he really had no choice in the matter, for the ad interim committee of the mission ordered him to proceed to the scene of the disorders to determine who was responsible for the violence. He most definitely did not go out seeking trouble, for if he had been left free to follow his own instincts he would have remained at Ibaanc safe from the Zappo Zap, whom he feared. What he discovered, however, was more than enough to poison relations between the State and the mission for over a decade.

Almost immediately after he commenced his tour of the ravaged area on September 13, 1899, Sheppard and his small party encountered an armed Zappo Zap patrol which, luckily for him, was led by a man whose life he had saved two years earlier. Together, they went to a campsite which reeked of decay near the village of Chinyama. When Sheppard beheld the Zappo Zap leader, M'lumba N'kusa, he believed that all his worst fears were about to be realized, for the chief was a devilish figure with his eyebrows shaven, his eyelashes plucked out, and his teeth filed to sharp points. Because he identified all foreigners with the Government, M'lumba freely confessed to Sheppard that he had been ordered by the State to collect tribute from "the Bakete, Bena Pianga and Bakuba and especially Lukenga's." [4]

For two days, Sheppard remained in the company of the armed raiders. During that time, the loquacious war chief vividly described how he had invited all of the Pianga village heads to his stockade and offered them the choice of paying the desired tribute or being killed. Since the imposition was excessive, most defaulted. Thereupon their villages were laid waste and perhaps between eighty to ninety of them were executed. Sheppard counted forty-one bodies and surmised that the rest had been eaten. He also viewed eighty-one hands being cured over a low fire. According to M'lumba, the State demanded the limbs as proof that he had completed his mission. [5]

Sheppard's graphic description of the carnage and cannibalism he had observed shocked his fellow evangelists. Because such barbarity was inconceivable to them, Lachlan Vass was dispatched to confirm the report. He counted fourteen incinerated villages and forty-seven corpses, some of them partially eaten. [6] For a distance of about 75 miles, he noted that the people had been compelled to take refuge in the bush despite the fact that it was during the rainy season. At one point, Hawkins complained, conditions became so

bad that "the safety, peace and progress" of the work at Ibaanc
were seriously jeopardized.[7]

In a desperate effort to prevent a repetition of such brutality,
Morrison personally rushed Sheppard's report to the State officials
at Luluabourg. In his opinion, it was not enough to punish the
actual raiders without taking action against the *chef de zone*
(DuFour) who authorized the violence. So much pressure was
ultimately applied by the evangelists that the administration reluctantly agreed to conduct a full-scale investigation of the affair. The
proceedings, however, were so patently biased that Morrison became permanently disenchanted with the Congo judiciary. In retrospect, it is conceivable that if the Government had made an honest
attempt to get at the truth, the A.P.C.M. might never have become
so deeply involved in the reform campaign.

The Presbyterians were particularly aggravated by the sectarian nature of the State rebuttal which was offered by Père Emeri
Cambier, *Supérieur de la Mission du Haut Kasai,* in the journals
La Métropole and *Le Congo Belge* in June 1900. According to the
Belgian priest, Sheppard's version of the affair was a complete
fabrication. Cambier maintained that not only had M'lumba N'kusa
acted on his own initiative, but it was he who was the victim of the
attack and not the Pianga.[8] Even the confession of the Zappo Zap
leader was held to have no significance, for it was seen as an effort
on his part to avoid punishment.

Cambier's testimony can be challenged on a number of
grounds. Most important of all, he was in Belgium when the raid
occurred, so he did not personally see what had happened; sec-
ondly, he was engaged in a bitter competition with the A.P.C.M.
for converts and therefore can hardly be considered objective; and,
lastly, he was indebted to the Zappo Zap, who had saved his life
when the Tetela garrison at Luluabourg had mutinied on July 4,
1895. Since the State was equally beholden to the Songye for their
aid in suppressing the rebels, it, too, overlooked some of their
egregious faults. After all, it was not exactly a secret that cannibalism was common among the Zappo Zap.

As was to be expected, the official investigation whitewashed
DuFour and all other local officers. On the basis of evidence

collected and the testimony heard, the advocate in charge concluded that the allegations of violence and extortion had been
greatly exaggerated. Since, according to his findings, the State was
not implicated in any way, DuFour was completely exonerated.
Even M'lumba N'kusa was set free after a few months to appease
the volatile Zappo Zap. To counter Morrison's charges, King
Leopold's aides wasted little time in making Washington aware
that the agents of the Free State had never been shown to be
responsible for any acts of cruelty.[9]

Yet most observers of the Congo scene, even Verner for that
matter, asserted that "black troops in the employ of the government did cut off the hands of natives, or otherwise abuse or
mutilate them." [10] The matter of controversy was whether the
administration actually ordered its troops to collect baskets full of
right arms, thus testifying to their punishment of shirkers. Certainly, State officials disclaimed any responsibility for such acts. In
response to those who charged otherwise, Leopold retorted: "Je
leur couperais bien tout le reste, mais pas les mains. C'est la seule
chose dont j'ai besoin au Congo!" [11] At the very least, however,
State officers must be blamed for creating the climate of violence
which had made such acts possible. Perhaps, as was the case
during the war against the Arab slavers, the Government became
so dependent upon the aid of its African allies, in this instance the
Zappo Zap, that it was powerless to interfere with their traditional
practices. As a consequence, the Songye indulged in cannibalism
and mutilation in the course of their campaign against the Pyaang.

Morrison, Vass, and Sheppard were combative personalities
who did not shrink from attacking officialdom. Unlike Grenfell,
who remained silent even after he was confronted with evidence of
the excesses of the *Force Publique,* they commenced to protest
vigorously. In fact, as soon as Morrison realized that the Government was seeking to shield its agents at the expense of the people's
best interests, he sent copies of Sheppard's testimony to Robert
Whythe in London with the request that he give the document
"such publicity as he may deem just." [12] The missionaries were
determined to arouse the conscience of the Christian world. Toward that end, they won the assistance of H. R. Fox Bourne, the

forthright Secretary of the Aborigines Protection Society, who incorporated Sheppard's account of the Zappo Zap raid in his polemic, *Civilization in Congoland.*

Morrison's opponents maintained that his protestations were not motivated solely by the revelation of the Zappo Zap outrages. Rather, they claimed that, in his thinking, selfish interests took precedence over humanitarian considerations. His intransigence was seen to stem from the unwillingness of the State to grant the Presbyterians as many mission sites as had been granted to the Catholics. To some extent, this may have been true, for the American missionaries were angered by the "restrictions and impediments" placed "in the way of Protestant evangelization." [13] Furthermore, Morrison did, in fact, visit the *commissaire* in Luebo to impress upon him the A.P.C.M.'s determination to secure additional concessions. However, just because Morrison and his colleagues were influenced by such considerations does not mean that they were not genuinely revolted by the horrors of the Zappo Zap raid and determined to protect the indigenous population from such a fate a second time.

Efforts by Government officials to intimidate the Presbyterian clerics and to frighten them into silence failed. Such attempts only stiffened them in their resolve to persevere in their criticism. To demonstrate the need for change, they unleashed a deluge of strongly worded charges which were designed to garner maximum publicity. In that way, they hoped to expose to the world the evils of Leopold's administration. If it had not been for the A.P.C.M., few people anywhere would have given any thought to the plight of the Congolese in the Kasai.

Whereas church leaders at home no longer possessed any confidence in the integrity of the Free State regime, they still entertained the belief that Leopold was a "wise and prudent ruler, and in every instance . . . a friend to the missions." [14] Blame for the disorders was placed on the shoulders of local officials. In part, the reluctance of the Mission Board to chide the king was due to the church's desire not to do anything that might encourage Belgium to annex the Free State at that time. The Presbyterians believed that, although he was a Catholic, heretofore he had shown himself to be very sympathetic to Protestants. Reservations were expressed, however, as to whether the "Protestant missions would fare as well under the direct control of Belgium." [15] Probably just such a thought moved Chester to write to Leopold to reaffirm the mission's good faith and humanitarian objectives and to state his personal hope that amicable relations could be maintained in the future.[16] In return, the Presbyterians expected the Belgian sovereign to order his officers in the Congo not to interfere with the enjoyment of their rights "under the General Act of the Berlin Convention in the matter of property concessions." [17]

Meanwhile in the United States, the members of the Executive Committee of the Board of World Missions found themselves in a quandary, for while they were anxious to protect the church's interests in the Congo, they were reluctant to see the mission become entangled in political affairs. Ultimately, they embarked upon two inevitably irreconcilable courses: they sought to retain King Leopold's good favor while simultaneously permitting denunciations of his agents to appear in the church press. In this way, they hoped to be able to exert pressure to bring about reforms without jeopardizing the mission's chances for expansion. Only such a dualistic policy could have brought about a situation whereby at the very same time that the Executive Committee was ordering its workers in the field "to observe all proper deference 'to the powers that be,' " [18] the church journal *The Missionary* was publishing a letter from Morrison charging that the Congo had "turned out to be a gigantic slave and trade company, whose philanthropy had been turned into greed." [19]

Chester did finally persuade his associates that the Zappo Zap raid transcended the political realm and warranted an appeal to the State Department, for the interests of American citizens in the Congo had been endangered. Of course, if he had really wanted to, he could still have tried to exclude the A.P.C.M. from the political arena by forbidding all public pronouncements on Congo affairs. Even at that late date, redress could have been sought through private approaches to King Leopold. Chester, however, had reached the point where he realized that it no longer was possible for him to say one thing while the men in the field said another.

His private assurances to Leopold carried no weight in the light of
Morrison's open denunciations. After the violent upheaval of
1899, Chester was more inclined to identify with those missionaries in the Kasai who were committed to a policy of direct action.
But whereas he tried to disguise the secular nature of his petitions
to Washington, Morrison and Vass recognized that even a humanitarian crusade was essentially political.

For that very reason, therefore, Vass didn't hesitate to call
upon the Aborigines Protection Society to use its influence to
induce the governments of Great Britain and the United States to
make representations on behalf of the Congolese in the same
manner that they had stood up for the rights of the Jews of Russia.
Certainly, he demanded that something be done without delay to
halt the "wild course of Leopold & his murdering crowd." While
asserting that he and his associates were still loyal to the Congo
Free State, Morrison let it be known that he was prepared to do
whatever was necessary to bring about the end of the villainous
state of affairs which then prevailed. Both men promised their full
support to the A.P.S. in its campaign to compel Leopold to live up
to the spirit of the Berlin Convention.[20]

NOTES

1. *The Missionary* (1893), p. 273. A letter from the Reverend D. C. Snyder,
March 27, 1893.
2. Slade, p. 306, n. 1, quoted from *A.P.C.M. Minutes,* June 8, 1897.
3. The A.P.C.M. was already frustrated, for the State had rejected its
applications for Kamba, Mukikamu, Boleke, and Lodji.
4. W. H. Sheppard, "Testimony with Respect to the Zappo Zap Raid," MS, p.
5, H.F.
5. *Ibid.,* pp. 6–7. He wanted 60 slaves, 10 fowl, 13 goats, 6 dogs, corn, *chumy,*
and rubber.
6. *The Missionary* (January 1900), p. 62.
7. *Ibid.*
8. *Le Congo Belge* (June 10, 1900), p. 183.
9. United States Legation, Belgium, to Secretary of State John Hay, July 19,
1902. *Dispatches of United States Minister to Belgium to State Department,
October 11, 1901, to December 19, 1903,* National Archives.
10. S. P. Verner, "Empire Building in Central Africa," ed. by Ralph Graves,
1907, MS, p. 64. An incomplete copy is included in the collection of Verner's
papers.
11. Colonel B. E. M. G. Stinglhamber and Paul Dresse, *Leopold II Au Travail*
(Brussels, 1945), p. 136. Leopold retorted that the last thing he would order to be
cut off would be the natives' hands, for he had use of them.

12. Morrison diary, October 23, 1899.

13. *The Missionary* (January 1900), p. 63.

14. *Ibid.* (June 1894), p. 237.

15. *Ibid.* (March 1901), p. 110.

16. Chester to King Leopold, March 15, enclosed in Chester to John Hay, March 16, 1900.

17. Samuel H. Chester, *Behind the Scenes* (Austin, 1928), pp. 78–79.

18. Slade, p. 306, n. 4, as quoted from Presbyterian Mission Minutes 9 1 1900.

19. *The Missionary* (February 1900), p. 66. A letter from Morrison dated November 15, 1899.

20. Vass to the A.P.S., November 3, 1902, and Morrison to the A.P.S., October 7, 1902, Aborigines Protection Society Papers, MSS Brit. Emp. S22 G261, Rhodes House, Oxford University.

6

The A.P.C.M. Role in the Reform Campaign in England and the United States

Before the reformers could bring the rapacious sovereign of the Congo to justice and convict him in the eyes of the world, they required concrete evidence of malfeasance. For, without such proof, they stood no chance of inducing the Signatories of the General Act of Berlin [1] to compel King Leopold to institute positive changes. Since there were no settlers in the Congo and the representatives of the rubber firms and the State profited from the regime,[2] it was left to the Protestant evangelists to denounce conditions in the colony, for they were the only ones with firsthand knowledge of the situation who were bold enough and willing to act.

To this day, there is still a spirited debate as to what really motivated men like Morrison to leap into the fray. In the partisan literature about the reform campaign, the clerics are either lauded as men of great moral courage combating the forces of mammon, or castigated as dupes or charlatans inspired by selfish designs, sectarian jealousy, and misguided zeal. Not surprisingly, the Belgian Catholics who dominated the Congo administration tended to view the Anglo-Saxon Protestant informants as foreign agents hostile to their interests. Actually, the missionaries were only responding to the people's wishes when they took an interest "in the political, economic and social affairs of the territories in which they operate[d]." [3] It must be conceded, however, that there were always a few churchmen who overdramatized what they saw in order to extract added financial support from their home boards, while a lesser number might have stretched the truth to satisfy the demands of the humanitarian societies for evidence. For the most part, however, the missionaries only reported what they saw or heard and allowed the facts to speak for themselves.

Much of the early clerical criticism of Leopold came from the American Baptists and Presbyterians stationed in the Congo. Perhaps this was so because their ties with Brussels were looser than those of the English missionaries. The latter had been allied with the Government in the bitter struggle to oust the Arabs and pacify the colony. This memory of joint suffering caused the English to hesitate before attacking the State. The Americans, on the other hand, tended to be more independent-minded and intolerant of restraint. It may have been because the United States was beginning to play a more aggressive role in the world. In the spirit of manifest destiny, the Presbyterians refused to allow any obstacles to stand in the way of their expansion. The A.B.M.U. was the first American mission to register a protest with the State Department in 1895 and the A.P.C.M. followed suit in 1900.

Because the evangelists did not choose to remain silent, Leopold's battery of propagandists did everything possible to discredit them. One of his spokesmen, Henry Wellington Wack, charged that the missions had been infiltrated by "quasi-political agents who believe that they find advantage in depreciating the Government." [4] According to Wack, the clerics went out of their way to "bring about the interference of their home Power in the affairs of the Government in whose territory they are labouring." [5] Samuel P. Verner was another who expressed reservations about the conduct of his former associates. He considered it most regrettable that they had violated Senator Morgan's solemn pledge to Leopold that they would not meddle in political affairs. Though he did acknowledge that Morrison was probably the most reliable of Leopold's adversaries, he nevertheless cuttingly commented that it was not necessary for "idealistic missionaries" to "leave Virginia to find Negroes abused." [6] Before the church presumed to lecture anyone else on race relations, he suggested that it put its own house in order. On the other hand, however, Verner's record was not as clean as it might have been, which leads one to suspect the genuineness of his concern for the fate of the Afro-American.

Morrison agreed that, ideally, missionaries ought not to become involved in political affairs. But under no circumstances would he abide by such a ban if a situation arose which threatened what he regarded to be the free exercise of fundamental human freedoms. Thus, at the first signs of systematic deprivations of life, liberty, and property, he urged his colleagues to take the following action:

    1. Give the natives wronged a letter to the nearest State official, politely requesting that justice be done, and the wrong be righted.

    2. Failing in this, a personal visit may be made or a personal letter may be addressed to the official.

    3. If this official has himself done the wrong or permits it to be done by soldiers or others under him, then let formal complaint be made to the superior officer of the district.

    4. Failing here of justice, appeal to Boma, and then to the Sovereign himself.

Only as a last resort, if all else had failed, did Morrison recommend public protest.[7]

The full measure of Morrison's influence in the reform campaign was not felt until his first leave. A recent assessment that it was Morrison "on his return to the United States by way of Europe in 1903, who was the pioneer of missionary agitation in England"[8] finds support in the testimony of Morrison's British allies. As one of them expressed it: "the gallant Virginian William Morrison turned up unexpectedly from the Congo . . . with a tale of continued infamy, with particulars of brutal and odious deeds; with a heart aflame with passion. There was nothing of the fanatic about him; no rhetoric; no invocations to the Deity; no prayerful entreaties. He was merely a capable, honest, strong, fearless man and he told his story with a moral force which thrilled all who heard it."[9]

His belligerent mood when he arrived in London testified in part to his resentment at being openly and boldly told by the Secretary of State for the Congo in Brussels, that henceforth no future concessions would be granted to the A.P.C.M. In order to bring pressure to bear on Leopold to force the king to remedy existing evils, Morrison had forwarded a written transcript revealing the true state of affairs in the Congo to the Conservative Foreign Secretary Lord Landsdowne. Subsequently, he sketched a verbal portrait of the wretched conditions in the Free State for the benefit of the Aborigines Protection Society. There were so many illustrious personages gathered to hear him deliver his talk at the Royal United Service Institute that it was mistakenly reported in some Presbyterian journals that he had addressed a joint session of the Commons and the Lords.

Morrison cited several instances of oppression and intimidation which had been witnessed by members of the A.P.C.M. between 1898 and 1902. He particularly emphasized the Zappo Zap raid to indicate how futile it was to expect any relief from the State. Since the judges were appointees of the Government, he maintained that they could not be trusted to correct matters.[10] Upon reflection, he concluded that the only solution was for an international panel to undertake an exhaustive investigation of Leopold's administration to determine whether he had, in fact, violated the General Act of Berlin.

In response to Morrison's impassioned plea for action, Charles Dilke moved "that this meeting having heard the statement of Rev. W. M. Morrison earnestly appeals to his Majesty's Government, as one of the Signatories to the Berlin and Brussels Acts of 1885 and 1892 [sic] to use its influence with the other Signatory Powers toward securing the humane and equitable treatment of natives in the Kongo Basin which was guaranteed by these Acts." [11] Moreover, within a matter of weeks, Herbert Samuel introduced a resolution in the House of Commons calling upon the British Government to take action which would insure justice in the Congo. Dilke had set virtually the same motion before the House six years earlier, but it had failed to get anywhere for want of popular support. Samuel enjoyed better luck in pressing the reform cause partly because Morrison's disclosures had aroused the public.[12]

Leopold realized that it was essential that Morrison's testimony be discredited, for the latter had damaged his position in England. To accomplish this purpose, he turned to Sir Hugh Gilzean Reid, an influential publisher and Baptist layman who had performed a similar function in the past. Indeed, Reid was so proud of his previous successes in this field that he boasted to Van Eetvelde that "one by one from Salusbury [sic] and Murphy to that Danish 'missionary' [Sjöblom] so-called, I have destroyed them and even stopped hostile criticism in our Parliament." [13] In an effort to add Morrison's scalp to his collection, Reid addressed a letter to the influential newspaper *Daily News* on May 11, countering each of the evangelist's assertions.

Another of Leopold's agents, C. H. der Hensler, who had been irritated at not being given the opportunity to answer Morrison in person at the Aborigines Protection Society meeting, seconded Reid's remarks. In essence, he accused Morrison, in the Belgian press, of being a fanatic who wished to establish his own fief in the Congo free of State control.[14] Amidst all the hyperbole, there was a kernel of truth in Hensler's statement. For, as legal representative of the mission, Morrison had objected so often and so hard to conscription, to compulsory labor, and to State taxes, which he considered inimical to the people's best interests, that it sometimes appeared that he believed that the Government could not do what he disapproved of.

After Reid and Hensler had fired off their salvos, the official Free State rejoinder was issued by M. Baert, the *chef de cabinet* in Leopold's regime. Baert demanded to know why Morrison had not lodged any complaints with the Government while he had been in Brussels. According to Baert, all that Morrison had discussed was the possibility of securing a concession for a mission site.[15]

Morrison publicly justified his silence, finally, by claiming that all his previous complaints had been ignored by the State. In retrospect, however, he admitted that he had erred in not pursuing the matter when he was in Brussels. Because his reputation had suffered from the charge that he had purposely avoided an examination of the facts, Morrison announced his willingness to confront Leopold in person with the same indictment that he had propounded in London. But his willingness to enter into the lion's den again was made contingent on the Free State's agreeing to pay all of his legitimate expenses, including transport and lodgings.[16] Not unexpectedly, the Secretary-General Ad. de Cuvelier angrily dismissed the evangelist's request that the authorities pay for his trip to Belgium. Instead, he advised him to use the mails, for the

Government, de Cuvelier averred, had no intention of subsidizing its critics.

Though he was in England only for a short time, Morrison touched the conscience of the public, and, what is more important, he encouraged many influential people to donate their energy and talents to the cause of reform. Because of that, as we have seen, his opponents did everything possible to discredit him. In the end, he managed to weather the storm of abuse which was directed at him and, with head unbowed, he departed for the United States in the hopes of winning American support for the campaign to oust Leopold. As the best means of doing that, he was anxious to forge an Anglo-American alliance, for unlike many of his fellow citizens, he was not an Anglophobe. Indeed, on the contrary, he deplored the wide currency of such views, for he wished to cement close ties between reformers in both countries.

Without doubt, Morrison's contribution to the reform campaign in both Britain and the United States was considerable. In large measure, he brought home to the people of both countries the reality of conditions in the Congo and made the public aware of the great need for a change. Because of this others were able to organize the opposition elements that he had aroused. Essentially, then, he provided the vital spark at the critical moment. As Dr. Robert Park, the Recording Secretary of the Congo Reform Association, acknowledged: "The campaign for reform of the Congo [was] precipitated in America by Rev. W. M. Morrison, a returned missionary of the Southern Presbyterian Church." [17]

Morrison had to plead his case in very strong and emotional terms, for the bitter aftermath of the Spanish-American War had made the American people and the administration wary of colonial involvement. Perhaps the most serious obstacle he had to overcome was the general lack of knowledge about Africa and what was going on in the Congo. In an effort to dispel that ignorance, Morrison wrote numerous articles in secular and religious journals, addressed countless church courts and congregations, and importuned several government leaders including the President. Elihu Root, who, when he was Secretary of State was one of those most

often approached by Morrison and his allies, afterward reflected
that:

> The very people who are most ardent against entangling alli-
> ances insist most fanatically upon our doing one hundred things
> a year on humanitarian grounds, which would lead to immediate
> war. . . . The Protestant Church and many good women were
> wild to have us stop the atrocities in the Congo. The fact we were
> parties to some earlier treaties gave some basis for an interest.
> . . . People kept piling down on the Department demanding
> action on the Congo. We went the limit which wasn't far.[18]

Though a clergyman, Morrison had a keen understanding of
power politics, and he was convinced that only if he could get the
various Protestant denominations to unite and to apply concerted
pressure on the President and Congress would he have any chance
to persuade Washington to intervene in the situation. In an effort
to bring about that end, he appealed to each church's sense of
humanity as well as to their intense fear and hatred of Catholicism.
A victory for Leopold, he warned, would be a defeat for the
Protestants. As it was, he claimed, the King and *Parlement* were
leagued with the Vatican in a "campaign of lies, cheap insults and
bluffing arrogance" which had as its objective the exclusion of all
Protestants from the Congo.[19]

To engage the sympathy of the American people, Morrison
cataloged the horrors he had witnessed in the Congo in a series of
polemical articles which appeared in such journals as the *Independent* and the *American Monthly Review of Reviews*. In a
typical piece, he described how he had "seen villages pillaged and
devastated and desecrated. . . . fifty thousand native people living
for weeks in the forests hiding from the outrages of this native
soldiery." As he anticipated, no one could help but be moved by
his account of how "helpless women and children of the villages
near to our mission station at Luebo fled into [his] house . . .
seeking protection." [20] In conclusion, he urged his readers to appeal to their representatives to bring pressure to bear on the
Government to use its good offices to relieve the burden of oppression. This was vital, he maintained, because the aggrieved Congolese by themselves simply could not bring about a change.

If nothing else, Morrison dispelled whatever lingering reservations some church leaders might still have entertained about the wisdom of becoming too deeply involved in this muckraking campaign. In the wake of his revelations, the Mission Board was prepared to exert the church's full measure of political leverage to protect the A.P.C.M.'s interests in the Kasai. As a first step, a committee was appointed in May 1903 and instructed to proceed to Washington to make the Government aware of the true state of affairs in the Congo. The delegates arrived in the capital in July, but accomplished very little, because the President and the Secretary of State were out of the city. With obvious reluctance, they presented their deposition to a State Department officer, promising to return in November in order to set the matter personally before Theodore Roosevelt and John Hay.

On November 7, Morrison and two of his associates did manage to confer with the Chief Executive. Although he professed to be deeply distressed by the dreadful evidence set before him, President Roosevelt made it quite clear that "the government would not be in a position to take any direct action in the case unless there was some specific instance of personal maltreatment of one of our American missionaries." In the event of such an occurrence, he pledged decisive steps would be taken to set things right.[21] What Morrison had hoped for was a realization on the part of the President of the obligation of his government to take decisive steps, since the United States had helped to facilitate Leopold's rule by being the first nation to grant recognition to the Free State. Though he was pleased by the consideration given his complaints, Morrison feared that very little would be done about them.

As it turned out, the State Department pursued the matter to the extent of ordering Lawrence Townsend, the American Minister in Belgium, to inquire about conditions in the Congo. Unfortunately, Hay might just as well have asked Leopold to investigate himself, for Townsend was most reluctant to jeopardize the good relations that existed between Brussels and Washington by asking too many questions about developments in Africa. His skepticism about the validity of the evangelists' charges was fed by Verner, who volunteered to look into the situation on his behalf when he returned to the Congo to collect curios for the Louisiana Purchase Exposition.[22] Because of his unfriendly opinions and questionable associations, Townsend was cordially disliked by the Presbyterian missionaries.

When the American mission boards became convinced that President Roosevelt did not intend to act and that petitions did not impress King Leopold, they resolved to seek the assistance of Congress. To that end, Dr. Thomas Barbour took the lead in convening a meeting of representatives of the A.B.M.U. (of which he was a member), the A.P.C.M., and the Foreign Christian Missionary Society. They met in Washington on March 23, 1904, and composed a memorial which Senator Morgan agreed, perhaps out of a sense of guilt for his earlier pro-Leopold activities or out of frustration that the Berlin Act had not been interpreted to encourage American Negroes to help uplift the Congolese, to present to the Senate. Whatever his reason, the *Memorial Concerning Conditions in the Independent State of the Kongo* was referred to the Senate Foreign Relations Committee of which he was then the ranking minority member.

The petition included Morrison's report to Lord Landsdowne, his address to the Aborigines Protection Society, other missionary briefs and extracts from the damning report of the British consul, Roger Casement. Essentially, what the framers [23] of the memorial contended was that the Powers had the right to act as official guardians of the indigenous population, for the Congo had acquired an international status through Leopold's acceptance of the General Act of Berlin. As was to be expected, such assertions only angered the king, for he considered the Berlin agreement to be nothing more than a declaration of general principles and intentions which were not binding and not enforceable. To those who claimed otherwise, he said: "My rights on the Congo are indivisible; they are the result of my personal labour and expense." [24] A good many legislators also professed to see no justification for the United States to get involved in the controversy. In rebuttal, Morrison emphasized that America had an overriding responsibility, as a member of the family of nations, to see to it that justice was done. What was more, the proponents of the memorial reminded the senators of America's participation in the Berlin talks and of the separate treaty with the Free State which guaranteed United States citizens liberty of conscience, the free exercise of worship, and the right to organize and to maintain missions.

The problem was not that American and British leaders did not realize what was going on in the Congo, but rather that either they did not want to get involved or they did not know how to proceed. Legal barriers aside, Britain was most reluctant to endanger its own position in Africa by reopening the question of the partition. Washington even went one step further by disclaiming any political interest at all in Africa and deferring in favor of London. Unfortunately, Britain's expressions of concern for the fate of the Congolese were dismissed by most people throughout the world as disguising the selfish aims of Perfidious Albion.

The propelling force behind the reform movement in Britain was Edmund Dene Morel, to whom A. J. P. Taylor fittingly referred as "the first Radical of the twentieth century who took up foreign affairs as a wholetime interest." [25] Like few other men, before or since, Morel was ideally suited to lead a crusade. He seemed to thrive on adversity and persevered where most others would have faltered. If the objective was the eviction of Leopold from Africa, then he concluded that the best way to go about it was to unite "in one body the various influences at work against Leopoldianism . . . to incorporate all men whose hearts were touched, whatever their standing, profession, political opinion and religious belief in a common aim." [26] At the suggestion of Roger Casement, Morel set up the Congo Reform Association on March 24, 1904, to accomplish this design.

In an effort to promote closer cooperation among all the reform groups, Barbour and Chester invited Morel to visit the United States. Since the British activists were just as anxious to effect stronger ties with their American allies, he accepted. Moreover, his associates thought the time ripe to present a petition to President Roosevelt. While he was in America, Morel hoped to be able to stimulate the creation of a collateral reform association. One of the obstacles in the path of such an organization, however, was the mistaken belief that the reform furor had been manufactured by the British Government to conceal its designs on the Congo.

Though Morrison favored Morel's visit, he did not agree that it was a propitious moment to approach the Chief Executive. As a matter of fact, he tried to persuade Morel to delay his trip until after the 1904 election, for Roosevelt, he shrewdly surmised, was "not anxious for disturbing elements to come in now that the campaign is on." [27] When Morel persevered in coming, despite Morrison's advice, Roosevelt affected a polite but disinterested air when he received him and the British ambassador on September 30.

As Morel recalled the meeting, he was "ushered into Mr. Roosevelt's presence as he sat at the head of a cabinet meeting discussing England's attitude in the matter of contraband in food-stuffs in time of war (the Russo-Japanese War was proceeding)." [28] He accepted the memorial which Morel presented to him, but aside from suggesting the possibility of raising the issue at a new Hague Conference he wasted little time in shunting it to the State Department for proper burial. Morel, however, was led to believe that the President would go into the whole question carefully and was given an appointment to see Secretary of State John Hay. But just two days earlier that same gentleman had confessed his view that it was "a well-meant impertinence, after all, for Englishmen to come to us to take up their Congo quarrel." [29]

According to Morel, though Hay professed to be favorably impressed with the strength and tone of the memorial, he maintained America's case was weak for not having signed the Berlin Act. What was more, he asserted, the United States had no material interest at stake and could not afford to become preoccupied with every humanitarian concern if the government was to be left sufficient time to conduct its proper affairs. When Morel suggested that American missionaries had been obstructed, Hay replied that they had failed to supply evidence of "specific instances of cases where they had been refused land, and otherwise interfered with." He did seem to have been impressed, in any case, with the violence of Morrison's language in describing conditions in the Congo. But since he could not permit emotion to take precedence over the law,

Hay would agree to say no more publicly than that the Government was keeping the matter under consideration. Privately, he told Morel: "while we keep it open, the effect must be good." [30] Morel received the impression, however, that Hay was reluctant to move for fear of disturbing the Catholics, most particularly the Irish, so soon before an election.[31]

Following his setback in Washington, Morel proceeded to Boston where he was to join Morrison in addressing the 13th International Peace Congress then in session there. Since the Congo issue figured to be the central theme in both their talks, Leopold was determined to do everything possible to prevent them from damaging his position any more than they had already done in the past. On the king's behalf, Cardinal Gibbons exerted heavy pressure on the sponsors of the meeting to deny Morel a forum at the conference. That powerful and highly respected Catholic prelate of Baltimore had been led to believe that the abuse heaped upon the king was all part of a Protestant conspiracy hatched by the British Government.

Leopold was so anxious to refute his adversaries that he dispatched six of his best agents to assist Gibbons at the meeting.[32] While they did their best to highlight the accomplishments of the Free State, a seventh agent, Henry I. Kowalsky, denounced the sponsors of the conference for allowing "a disgruntled American missionary [Morrison?] to whom concessions in the Congo were refused . . . inveigh against the government without restrictions." [33] Even the Belgian Ambassador, Baron Ludovic Moncheur, contrived to do his part by arranging for the *North American Review* to incorporate his own glowing account of "Conditions in the Congo Free State," in its October issue.

Leopold had good reason, as it turned out, to fear the impact of Morrison and Morel's words, for by the time they sat down almost everybody in the audience was of the opinion that the Free State regime was one of "the most heartless and iniquitous in the history of modern colonization enterprises." [34] As a result, the delegates resolved to ask either for a renewed conference of the Berlin Powers or for an international commission of inquiry to answer the questions:

1. . . . . [is] the government of the Congo Free State still to be regarded as the trustee of the Powers which recognized the flag of the International Association?

2. If not, what is the position of the Congo Free State in international law, and in what manner may the grave questions concerning its alleged actions be satisfactorily and competently determined? [35]

One added dividend of Morel's trip was the establishment of a Congo Reform Association in Boston in November 1904. Though it was patterned after the older British organization, business interests played a less important role and the clergy assumed a far heavier share of the propaganda effort. The Southern Presbyterians gave the C.R.A. their full support, but the Northern Baptists provided the leadership of the group which had its headquarters in Tremont Temple in Boston.

Efforts by Leopold to disarm his critics by pretending an interest in the fate of the Congolese people drew derision from his antagonists. Indeed, when he appointed a so-called international panel to investigate the validity of Casement's charges of brutality and exploitation, Morrison expressed the sentiments of a legion of doubters when he wrote Morel that "old man Leopold is in a trot now trying to wash his 'dirty linen' out in the Congo. You may depend on it there wont [sic] be much real washing done—just a little starch smeared on the outside. Leopold would have to wash himself before he could expect to make progress washing anyone else." [36]

Meanwhile, the General Assembly of the Presbyterian Church in the United States once again petitioned Washington in May 1906:

to bring about by any means that may be practicable an immediate concert of action on the part of all civilized nations, and particularly of those nations participating in the Berlin Convention, establishing the Congo Independent State, to abate the atrocities which have been and are being committed on the natives, and to grant to all nations and particularly to Protestant missions, free access to all parts of the State for the establishment of missions. [37]

As was usually the case, the clerics weakened their position by combining an appeal for just treatment of the Congolese with a plea for equal rights for themselves. Thus it could be charged that they were motivated by nothing more than greed and jealousy.

Despite their lack of success in the past, the Presbyterian and allied missionary boards continued to bombard the State Department with letters demanding prompt action. Regardless of the pressure and of his own private feelings, Secretary of State Elihu Root was determined to keep the United States out of the affair. In response to a request from Congressman Denby that he expedite consideration of the Morgan Memorial, he emphasized that America had no political interests in Africa and was not even a signatory of the General Act of Berlin. Moreover, he frankly confessed that "if the United States had happened to possess in Darkest Africa a territory seven times as large and four times as populous as the Philippines, we, too, might find good government difficult and come in for our own share of just or unjust criticism." [38]

Much of the press supported his position. The *New York Tribune,* for instance, contended that every nation must be left free to chart its own domestic course without outside interference. If the United States asserted the right to intervene in the Congo, then, the *Tribune* asked, what was to stop Belgium from claiming jurisdiction over cases of lynching in the South? [39] These isolationist sentiments were warmly applauded by Free State apologists who considered the "Denby letter" to be a victory for their side in the battle to influence the American government.

Chester and Morrison, however, contended that just the opposite was ultimately the case. In their opinion, Root was so shocked by the flood of protest mail which deluged him from unexpected sources following the publication of the letter that he determined to assign an American consul to the Free State to report on what was really going on there. Furthermore, he pledged to Chester that "he would interpret the Treaty between the U.S.A. and the Congo Independent State as giving [the A.P.C.M.] the right to demand necessary land concessions for the organization and maintenance of our Missions." [40] Chester was particularly gratified by the appointment of an American consul, for he anticipated that this might be the means of finally bringing the United States "into collision with that monster, the Congo Independent State." [41]

To prevent such an end, great sums of money were expended by Leopold to convince people that he had been unfairly maligned by deceitful men. An international network of paid agents, some professional and some amateur, pictured the reform campaign as "an attempt of England to bully Belgium and perhaps deprive her of a hard won colonial territory" or alternatively as an "overt attack of the Protestant missionaries on a Catholic government." [42] A mixed chorus of voices demanded to know in many languages why the Free State had been singled out for criticism, when forced labor and heavy taxes could be found in every colony. If the other imperial powers could seize vacant lands and charter concessionary companies without complaint, why couldn't Leopold, his advocates asked. Was it not strange, they noted, that when the king had been struggling just to keep the venture going that not a reproachful word had been heard.

Of course, the critical difference was that none of the other colonies had been transformed into strictly commercial enterprises wherein everybody and everything was sacrificed for the purpose of securing the maximum immediate profit at the least expense. Their riches did not flow entirely to one man and a few chosen companies. No doubt the stronger nations got away with some of the things for which Leopold was being criticized, but their regimes were not noted exclusively for their brutality and bloodshed.

For a man who was so quick to heap abuse upon his enemies, Morrison was surprisingly sensitive to any aspersions cast on his own character. Thus he reacted angrily to the machinations of the "Congo crowd" to undermine his reputation. What particularly aggravated him was that they did not come out and fight in the open like "honest Americans." Rather, he charged, they went about serving the interests of the Free State in the guise of innocent travelers and disinterested observers.

No one irritated him more than the Beglian Ambassador. On the one occasion that he met Moncheur at Warm Springs, he "found him thoroughly saturated with greed & inflated with the idea the Congo State was absolutely independent and nobody could do anything—the State had [the] right to do as it pleased." [43] Though he dismissed him as a poor, ignorant fellow who was a captive of his own propaganda, Morrison was sufficiently annoyed to protest Moncheur's actions to Root. He specifically objected to the attempt of the diplomat to make it appear as if every attack on the Free State was also a criticism of Belgium. [44]

Of all the people who became involved in this war of words, Samuel Phillips Verner was undoubtedly the most enigmatic. Because of his past association with the A.P.C.M., his activities were of more than passing interest to the reformers. Indeed, Morrison warned Morel that "for good and sufficient reasons, which it is perhaps not necessary for me to mention now, he [Verner] is not now, in any way connected with our mission & we are in no way responsible for him." He added "some doubt the man's sanity, but this you need not refer to, of course." [45] Senator Morgan received an anonymous letter, much in the same vein, charging "Verner was withdrawn from the Congo mission by the Presbyterian Board on account of his conduct and personal life. After his return to America he spent some time in a private sanitarium for mental trouble." [46] And even earlier, when Phipps placed his trust in Verner, Roger Casement expressed his view that he was "a bore" whom everyone thought was "cracked." [47] What was more, he passed on the opinion of Lawson Forfeitt of the Baptist Missionary Society who thought that Verner was "somewhat peculiar" due to perhaps having been affected by the sun. [48]

None of the several explanations Verner offered for leaving the mission related to either his conduct or his mental condition. He claimed that he had accepted the position of business manager on the understanding that it was to be only a temporary appointment and that he would have ample freedom to explore the possibilities of commercial development and scientific study. In his book *Pioneering in Central Africa,* in which he recounted his experiences, he asserted that his service was cut short by a severe leg injury which required prolonged hospitalization in the United States. Essentially, Verner maintained that he was compelled to abandon the spiritually rich but materially poor life of an evangelist because his illness and subsequent marriage left him in need of greater funds.

In reality, Verner was considered undeserving of reappointment. Such a conclusion seems logical in light of the fact that he was reproved on more than one occasion for "the spirit of insubordination" which sometimes found expression in his letters. What particularly aggravated his superiors was his "opening of a new station [Ndombe] without either conference or permission from the Committee." To show their displeasure, they sternly warned him that in future he was not to act contrary to the code of behavior set down in the mission manual.[49] In the end, however, despite the A.P.C.M.'s critical need of workers, Chester ordered him home when he persisted in acting independently. Though health was the stated reason for his recall and he had, indeed, injured himself, it is doubtful whether he would have been allowed to remain in the field even if he had been in perfect physical condition. In the words of Snyder, "as a missionary he was a decided failure." [50]

Whereas Verner's statements in support of King Leopold infuriated the reformers, they delighted Baron Moncheur. So much so, in fact, that he ventured all the way to St. Louis to seek Verner's advice and cooperation. Later, when Verner returned from his second trip to the Congo, Moncheur sent him a confidential letter expressing official approval of his plan to establish an institute of technology in the Wissmann Falls region. This was intended to compensate him for all that he had done in "the defense of the just cause of the Congo against prejudiced and unfair criticism." It was too bad, Moncheur commented, that the public paid more attention to the trash of the missionaries "than it does to a fine letter like your last one, because it is signed with a pseudonym." Particularly noteworthy was the fact that the Belgian Ambassador promised Verner favorable treatment in the Congo, if he agreed to make a series of speeches defending the Free State. While he was to pretend to be an impartial observer, his tour was to be subsidized by Leopold.[51] Yet even after this, Verner had the gall to maintain that he was "no apologist for King Leopold and no advocate of any particular interest." [52]

In many ways, Verner was a peculiar case, for he condemned

the labor, revenue, and land policies of the Free State while at the same time lauding the king. He admitted that violence and oppression characterized the system, but he pretended that it was unavoidable. While he was concerned about the welfare of the Congolese, he was more interested in satisfying his economic ambitions. Because none of his projects could be implemented without the approval of the State, Verner became a partisan defender of the Government. Thus while he pretended to be objective, he was nothing of the sort. He was even willing to denounce his former colleagues when they sided with Leopold's opponents. And in return, they, of course, did everything possible to blacken his character and question his stability.

At a critical point in the struggle for reform, the *New York American* began a series of articles exposing the nefarious workings of Leopold's lobby in the United States. The paper claimed to have gleaned its information from the documents of Colonel Henry Kowalsky, who was identified as the head of the propaganda operation. The unmasking of the covert network largely negated its effectiveness and substantially weakened Leopold's position in America. Though he asserted he was not influenced by the disclosures, Senator Henry Cabot Lodge introduced a resolution in Congress calling for an international investigation of conditions in the Congo just a few hours after the story broke.[53] The passage of his resolution, albeit in a milder form due to the lobbying of Moncheur on February 15, 1907, was one indication which, when added to the diplomatic overtures to Britain to coordinate action, showed that Washington had finally decided to move beyond its previous cautious policy of concerned detachment.

In concert with Britain, the United States began to apply increasing pressure on Belgium to annex the Congo. Though such a solution seemed satisfactory to the reformers, they wished to make certain that substantial improvements would result from the change in sovereignty. Chester took great pains to impress this point upon Root. Perhaps, more than anything else, the missionaries wanted assurances that every official "trained" by Leopold in brutality and oppression would be immediately removed. Unless the heavy hand of the Belgian monarch was completely lifted from

the Congo, Morrison foresaw little change. It would be "like
cutting off a twig, expecting thereby to kill the poisonous tree." [54]

In the past, there had been very little enthusiasm in Belgium
for the idea of ruling the Congo Free State. Both in 1895 and
1901, the Government had clearly demonstrated that it preferred
not to assume the burden of administering the costly and unstable
colony. By 1906, however, following the critical report of King
Leopold's commission of inquiry and his subsequent condemnation
by two Belgian writers, Père Arthur Vermeersch and Félicien
Cattier, whose findings could not be held to be dictated by foreign
bias, most Belgians came to the conclusion that something had to
be done to improve conditions in the colony. The growing discon-
tent of the people and the intensification of Anglo-American pressure led Brussels to consider the possibility of assuming control of
the Free State. In the end, the ruling Catholic party was reluctantly
forced to pursue this course, as were most Liberals. Even the
Socialist leader, Emile Vandervelde, agreed, although his party
was not prepared to go along with him. Serious discussion of the
problem dragged from late 1906 through 1907 without anything
much being accomplished until the parliamentary debates of April
1908. Leopold saw that he had no choice but to surrender the
Congo, but agreement was delayed by his determination to re-
ject any settlement that was not completely to his liking. Finally,
after much haggling, the transfer was approved by the Belgian
Chamber and Senate in the summer of 1908. The king signified his
assent on October 18th, and Brussels assumed full control of the
dependency the next month.

Though the Presbyterians publicly welcomed the "transfer
from a piratical, irresponsible despotism to an honorable responsible enlightened liberty-loving nation," [55] many members of the
mission were unhappy that Protestant Britain or even the United
States had not annexed the territory. Initially, most of their reservations related to religious concerns, for the Calvinists were uncer-
tain as to how they might fare under Belgian rule. For that reason,
Morrison urged Chester to remain alert "if the state is to be taken
over by Belgium, to see to it that our religious rights are preserved,

for you know that Belgium is one of the most bigoted Roman Catholic countries in Europe." [56]

Later, when the actual terms of the cession became known, the Presbyterians were outraged, for the *Charte Coloniale* preserved all existing legislation and upheld the legality of the monopoly concessions. To make matters worse, the old officials were retained to administer the objectionable laws. All in all, as far as the reformers were concerned, very little had changed. Chester, therefore, implored the State Department to defer recognition of the annexation until after reforms had become a reality. Even earlier, Root had strongly urged the Belgian Government to introduce measures which would, among other things, exempt Africans from excessive taxation, forbid forced labor, emancipate the judiciary, and permit free trade and settlement everywhere. [57] When such action was not taken immediately, both Washington and London indicated their displeasure by refusing to recognize the change in administrations.

Morrison, in particular, was sorely disappointed by this turn of events. While he had anticipated that Belgium might minimize the errors of Leopold's administration, he had hardly expected Brussels to defend the king's discredited regime. At the very least, he believed that Belgium would have the good sense to remove some of the worst offenders. Probably, most disappointing of all, he resented being viewed as a greater menace than the men he exposed. As an expression of their displeasure, the evangelists escalated their demands for redress, but now they focused their fire on the operations of the Compagnie du Kasai which had been leagued with Leopold in his exploitation of the province. Since Belgium inherited the monarch's half-ownership of the concern, the battle promised to be a tough one.

NOTES

1. The nations represented at the Berlin Conference were: England, Italy, France, the United States, Germany, Russia, Austria-Hungary, Spain, Sweden, the Low Countries, Portugal, Norway, Turkey, and Denmark. The United States, however, did not sign the General Act.

2. Moreover, to compel their silence the State withheld one-half of their wages in Brussels until the termination of their service and did not hesitate to deny medical supplies and transport to talkative employees.

3. Adjei, pp. 196–197.

4. H. W. Wack, *The Story of the Congo Free State* (New York, 1905), p. 307.

5. *Ibid.,* p. 464.

6. Verner to Root, December 10, 1906.

7. W. M. Morrison, "Under What Circumstances are we Justified in making public the accounts of Atrocities and other forms of injustice to the Natives," *Report of the United Missionary Conference on the Congo* (1907), p. 97.

8. Slade, p. 307.

9. William Roger Louis and Jean Stengers, *E. D. Morel's History of the Congo Reform Movement* (Oxford, 1968), pp. 125–126. Actually, Fox Bourne knew of Morrison's coming months ahead of time, though Morel did not learn his identity till the last moment.

10. On one occasion the Vice-Governor-General became so outraged by Morrison's imputations against King Leopold that he warned him to adopt "une attitude plus en concordance avec l'hospitalité et la liberté qui vous sont garanties dans ce pays." Wangermée to Morrison, January 26, 1903, enclosed in Fox Bourne to Foreign Office, July 3, 1903, F.O. 10/805.

11. Senate Document 282, 58th Cong., 2nd Sess., *Memorial Concerning Conditions in the Independent State of the Kongo,* presented by Senator Morgan and referred to the Committee on Foreign Relations on April 19, 1904, p. 42.

12. The Foreign Office, however, was only willing to concede that Morrison's testimony added weight to the impression that the implementation of compulsory military service and forced labor was attended with much brutality. Because much of the evidence was hearsay and the cases were some years old, his brief was not thought to be sufficient to provide the basis for an indictment against the Free State.

13. Slade, p. 251, n. 4, quotes Reid to Van Eetvelde 6 XII 97. A.G.R., V.E. 19. Reid was an officer in the Order of Leopold and Knight Commander of the Order of the Crown. Murphy and Sjöblom, who was Swedish, were members of the A.B.M.U.

14. *Mouvement Géographique* (May 31, 1903), p. 276, quoted from *L'Etoile Belge.*

15. J. Boillot-Robert, *Leopold II Et Le Congo* (Neuchâtel, 1903), p. 28. This revelation was undoubtedly damaging though in defense of Morrison it might be said that he was acting in response to the advice of the American Minister in Brussels who warned him that he might prejudice his chance for a concession if he raised other matters. See Phipps to Landsdowne, May 15, 1903, F.O. 10/803.

16. Morrison to Leopold, June 20, 1903, enclosed in Townsend to Hay, July 14, 1903. Correspondence United States Legation, Belgium to Department of State, 1901–1903.

17. Robert E. Park, "Leopold II King of Belgium and Captain of Industry: A Character Sketch," MS (1907), p. 4. Missionary Research Library, New York.

18. Philip C. Jessup, *Elihu Root, 1905–1937* (New York, 1938), II, 61–62.

19. Morrison, "Under What Circumstances," pp. 99–100.

20. Morrison, "Personal Observations of Congo Misgovernment," *The American Monthly Review of Reviews,* XXVIII (July 1903), 39.

21. Chester, p. 82. President Roosevelt had a copy of *Red Rubber,* by E. D. Morel, on his desk when he received the committee.

22. At Townsend's urging, Sir Constantine Phipps met Verner and found him to be informed and wholly impartial. While claiming to be on good terms with Morrison, he described his actions in the United States as being "ill-judged,

exaggerated, and injurious to missionary interests." Phipps to Landsdowne, January 6, 1904, F.O. 403/351.

23. Henry C. Mabie, home secretary of the A.B.M.U.; Thomas B. Barbour, foreign secretary of the A.B.M.U. and chairman of the Board of American Foreign Missions; S. H. Chester, W. M. Morrison, and D. C. Snyder of the A.P.C.M.; Archibald McClean, president of the Foreign Christian Missionary Society; and E. A. Layton of the F.C.M.S.

24. *La Vérité sur la Congo* (June 30, 1906), p. 261. A letter from Leopold dated June 30, 1906.

25. A. J. P. Taylor, *The Troublemakers: Dissent over Foreign Policy, 1792–1939* (London, 1957), p. 119.

26. W. R. Louis, "Roger Casement and the Congo," *Journal of African History*, V, No. 1 (1964), p. 115, quoted from Morel's "History of the Congo Reform Association." In condemning the system which he believed inevitably led to atrocities, Morel based his attack on four pillars: human pity, British honor, international commercial rights, and native economic and personal liberties.

27. Morrison to Morel, June 16, 1904, in the papers of E. D. Morel in the British Library of Political and Economic Science, London. Hereafter cited as M.P.

28. Morel to Walter Langley, February 26, 1909, M.P.

29. *The Letters of Theodore Roosevelt,* selected and edited by Elting Morrison (Cambridge, 1951), LV, Roosevelt to Eugene Philbin, September 28, 1904.

30. Report of The Honorary Secretary of The Congo Reform Association, On His Visit To the United States, M.P.

31. Morel to Lord Fitzmaurice, December 24, 1905, M.P.

32. Dr. Charles Sarolea, who served as his consul in Edinburgh; George Herbert Head, R.A., of Cambridge, England; Professor Nerincx of the University of Louvain and George Washington University; James Gustavus Whiteley of Baltimore; a Mr. Mansfield, who was the Belgian consul in Boston; and Carton de Wiart, who was a Belgian senator and the brother of Leopold's private secretary. Gibbons himself was not present.

33. Kowalsky to Barbour, November 16, 1904, M.P.

34. Vinson, p. 186.

35. *Ibid.,* p. 53.

36. Morrison to Morel, June 16, 1904, M.P. Because of the pressure exerted by the British Foreign Office and the reformers, Leopold was compelled to give the commission an international cast and grant it wider latitude than he would have preferred.

37. Presbyterian Church in the United States to the State Department, May 1906, Numerical File 1906–1910, Cases 1797/350-1806/79, No. 191. Hereafter cited as S.D. 191.

38. *House Document 565,* 59th Cong., 1st Sess., p. 2, quoted in Jessup, pp. 62–63.

39. *La Belgique Coloniale et Maritime* (March 18, 1906), p. 369.

40. Chester to Morel, April 28, 1906, M.P.

41. Chester to Morel, July 23, 1906, M.P.

42. Park, p. 5.

43. Morrison to Morel, August 16, 1904, M.P.

44. Morrison to Root, February 22, 1906.

45. Morrison to Morel, November 1, 1904, M.P. Morel indicated that Verner would have to be discredited if he continued to issue statements supporting Leopold.

46. Anonymous letter to Morgan, January 8, 1907, Morgan Papers, Library of Congress.

47. Casement to Farnell, February 18, 1904, F.O. 10/808. Casement acted as the American consul in the Congo when he served as the British representative there.

48. Casement to F.O., January 18, 1904, F.O. 10/807.

49. The Reverend R. C. Rees to Verner, September 14, 1897, Verner Papers. Rees was chairman of the Committee of Foreign Missions.

50. Extract of a letter from Snyder, February 4, 1904, enclosed in Casement to Farnell, February 18, 1904, F.O. 10/808.

51. Moncheur to Verner, December 20, 1904, V.P.

52. Verner to Root, November 20, 1906, Kongo Minor File, No. 34. Verner may not have invested his money in the Congo, but he was active in the organization of the American Congo Company. He even led an exploratory expedition for the firm.

53. Root informed the British Minister in Washington that Lodge had not acted at the behest of the Department of State, but in response to the pressure exerted by his constituents in Massachusetts where missionary interest was strong. Sir M. Durand to Sir E. Grey, December 13, 1906, F.O. 367/33.

54. Morrison, *Protestant Missionary Conference, 1907*, p. 8.

55. *Kasai Herald* (January 1909), p. 8.

56. Vinson, p. 76.

57. Wilson to Davignon, April 7, 1908, *Documents Diplomatiques*, p. 59. He justified his intervention by citing America's signing of the Brussels Act.

7

The Compagnie du Kasai
v. Morrison and Sheppard

The second stage of the reform struggle saw the A.P.C.M. locked in combat with the rubber lords who were trying to extract "the cream of the country" [1] before Belgium assumed control. Not surprisingly, the conflict intensified following the return of Morrison to the field in October 1906. None of the evangelists, least of all Morrison, was prepared to sit by idly while the people's spirit was crushed by the oppressive rubber regime. As he described the scene to Chester, on the eve of annexation, "we are not now suffering from the old forms of outrage so much—handcutting, slave-raiding, murdering, etc.—but . . . I believe the sum total of suffering is much more than it was formerly." [2] Apparently a more subtle, less violent system of exploitation had been substituted for the blatant victimization of past years. As one missionary put it to Morel, "we have not had any very serious abuses by the Company near us, but out where we cannot see there are complaints coming in from the natives." [3] For Morrison, it was nothing less than a contest between the forces of civilization and brutalization, Christ and Satan. He was determined that Christ and the Congolese should triumph and that Leopold and his allies should be driven from the colony.

In an effort to siphon off the great wealth of the Congo, Leopold had declared the collection and distribution of rubber and ivory to be State monopolies. However, to win the silence of the free trade lobby, he did agree to a compromise whereby competitive commerce was preserved in the Kasai. This decision explains why there were so few Presbyterian complaints prior to 1906, although Luebo was surrounded by lush rubber forests. Elsewhere conditions deteriorated much more rapidly. Because it was one of the few havens left for small traders, twelve new firms commenced operations in the Kasai between 1894 and 1900. In a free market, their spirited competition caused wages to spiral appreciably.

At length, Leopold became dissatisfied with this arrangement, for not only was he not sharing in the Kasai profits but as well most of the competing firms in the province were failing financially. Thus the king determined to terminate competition and to that end he used his absolute powers to force all the Kasai firms to merge into one, termed the Compagnie du Kasai. The C.K. did not receive a concession of land, but it was granted the right to collect rubber, copal, and other products of the soil. Though not technically a monopoly, nevertheless the C.K. was guaranteed a free hand for thirty years. One immediate result of the amalgamation was that the Congolese were paid less and thus were not so eager to work for the Europeans. But since the economy rested on their backs, they were not permitted to withdraw from the labor mart. Defenders of compulsory toil like Victorien Lacourt, the *administrateur-directeur général* of the C.K., conveniently confused cultural advancement with coolie labor when they claimed that work was the best means of civilizing the African.

That the Compagnie du Kasai and the A.P.C.M. would come into conflict was almost predetermined. As a matter of fact, the strained relationship between the merchants and the missionaries predated the introduction of the rubber regime. Quite early in his evangelical career Morrison concluded that it was a certainty "that the traders either directly or indirectly oppose us at every point." [4] Only occasionally, however, were there any overt difficulties as when Mr. Hohman of the Dutch trading firm Nieuwe Afrikaanische Handels Vennootschaap intruded onto the mission grounds at Ibaanc and beat several missionary employees. A similar incident occurred at Luebo where Mr. Van den Hodel, whom Morrison considered "a crazy duck," refused to cooperate in easing tensions between the mission boys and the boys of the Dutch mercantile establishment. [5]

For the most part, however, the friction between the merchants and the evangelists was a reflection of their disparate life-styles and objectives. It was simply impossible for the abstemious missionaries who preached the sanctity of holy wedlock while dedicating themselves to the saving of souls to get along with the traders who ordinarily drank to excess, maintained several concubines, and thought of nothing but profit. Then to further aggravate matters, the offending merchants were generally Catholics or atheists.

Still, the A.P.C.M. did manage to coexist peacefully with the C.K. in the beginning. During that period, the Presbyterians were primarily concerned with ousting Leopold. But as soon as the base purposes and unscrupulous methods of the C.K. became common knowledge, the mission spared no effort to eliminate the "Twentieth Century slavery" imposed by the Company under the threat of death.[6] The brutal reality of how Company and State representatives conspired to despoil the people of the Kasai was revealed by the commission of inquiry set up by Leopold.

Much to his chagrin, his three handpicked investigators [7] documented the manner in which the inhabitants of the Sankuru basin were exploited. The State, they asserted, did its part by levying a tax which had to be paid in *croisettes*. Since these copper St. André crosses could only be secured from C.K. factors in return for India rubber, the Congolese were obliged to toil for the commercial concern. To complete the cycle, the State then promptly returned all the crosses that it had received to the C.K. Thus though the firm was not authorized to collect imposts, it was able to manipulate the tax system to draft the workers it needed. The Presbyterian evangelists were particularly disturbed, for they believed that the C.K. made the Protestant villages shoulder a disproportionate share of the burden.

Though the Company tried to prove that the commission was irresponsible and misinformed, it did not ignore the charges of the commissioners. The directors insisted that the tax in *croisettes* was older than the C.K. and they denied ever trying to monopolize the supply. On the contrary, the crosses were held to be available in great numbers in Katanga and Pania Mutombo. It was admitted that porterage existed, but only because there were no beasts of burden or mechanical devices that could be used to transport the rubber from the forests over almost invisible trails to company depots. As soon as it was feasible, the Company pledged that it would eliminate the practice. Skeptics, like Rochester and Martin, who questioned how profits could continue to rise while the supply of rubber was diminishing, were assured by Lacourt that it was due to the quality of the product and the stability of the world market.

More than anything else, the Compagnie du Kasai resented the fact that the commission of inquiry had based its condemnation of the firm's operations on its observation of the practices of other concerns. Equally disturbing to the management was the failure of the report to identify witnesses or document specific instances of oppression. Because the commission had acted in this manner, Lacourt accused the members of conspiring with Belgium's enemies in an attempt to facilitate the seizure of the Congo by Britain.[8] But since Leopold had appointed each one of them, such a conclusion defies logic. All this testifies to the fact that conditions were so bad that even royal investigators were appalled by the scenes which they beheld.

Nothing aggravated the Presbyterians more than the Company's shocking maltreatment of the Kuba, who obstinately declined to collect rubber. Not even the abandonment of the *croisette* system spared them, for the 40 hour a month labor tax was interpreted in such a manner as to compel each village to satisfy a rubber quota or see its residents fined, flogged, or imprisoned. According to Vass, "the people [were] being oppressed and killed" and "the resources of the country . . . destroyed . . . all for a few unprincipled dogs led by a disolute [sic] whoremunger [sic]."[9]

Vass was not the only one who was disturbed by the deterioration of conditions. Before the Company's pressure intensified, Morrison and Sheppard had been pleased to comment favorably on the clean orderly villages which they saw when they visited Mushenge in 1904. All about them, they confessed to seeing vast cornfields, bountiful acres of manioc, peanuts, and vegetables, and large numbers of fowl and goats. But then on the eve of Belgium's assumption of sovereignty, the C.K. stubbornly tightened its noose about the neck of the Kuba in order to squeeze out one last, great rubber harvest. What happened as a result was movingly described by Sheppard in the January 1908 issue of the *Kasai Herald*.

Whereas just three years earlier, he recalled, the Kuba had been happy, healthy, and strong, all that had changed. Now, he reported:

> Their farms are growing up in weeds and jungle, their king is practically a slave, their houses now are mostly only half-built single rooms, and are much neglected. The streets of their towns are not clean and well swept as they once were. Even their children cry for bread.
>
> Why this change? You have it in a few words. There are armed sentries of chartered trading companies who force the men and women to spend most of their days and nights in the forests making rubber, and the price they receive is so meagre that they cannot live upon it. In the majority of villages these people have not time to listen to the Gospel story, or give an answer concerning their soul's salvation.[10]

To protect their interests and silence their critics, Company officers felt impelled to go on the offensive. Under ordinary circumstances, they would have preferred to have remained silent, but they no longer could afford such a luxury, for it would have been interpreted as a confession of guilt. The last straw was the publication of Sheppard's stark account of the plight of the Kuba. It made no difference to them that Sheppard had not mentioned the C.K. by name, for their object was to forestall future attacks by means of discrediting their clerical opponent.

A British observer later suggested that the Compagnie du Kasai decided to bring an ill-faith charge against Sheppard out of a feeling of betrayal that he should have authored such an article. According to the consul, Sheppard had previously "resisted all Dr. Morrison's entreaties to attack King Leopold's methods of administration, and was invariably silent on this subject when on furlough in America, on account of the social hatred produced by the colour question in that country." [11] Thus when he finally gave in to Morrison's repeated requests that he aid in the campaign and published his story in the *Kasai Herald,* the Company reacted bitterly. But such an explanation fails to take into account Sheppard's leading role in the Zappo Zap affair and betrays an ignorance of Morrison's responsibility as legal representative of the mission to pass on the complaints of his colleagues. Moreover, since the charges against Sheppard were not brought until a year after the article appeared, it would seem that other factors influenced the decision of the directors.

None of the evangelists, not even Sheppard or Vass, was more constant or abrasive in his denunciations of the Compagnie du Kasai than Morrison. Without apparent fear of consequence, he excoriated the firm's executives in the letters he exchanged with them. Dr. Dreypondt, who directed the field operations of the concern between 1902 and 1908, initiated the correspondence by demanding that the A.P.C.M. print a retraction of Sheppard's accusations in the *Kasai Herald*. According to him, the C.K. employed "only one single trading principle—that of supply and demand and the natives are not forced to make rubber for us or to do any other work." [12] Such an apology was ruled out of the question by Morrison unless Sheppard was proven wrong by an impartial international panel.

In his reply, Louis Napoleon Chaltin, who succeeded Dreypondt, hinted that he might be willing to entertain the prospect of a formal inquiry, if the allegations of wrongdoing were made more precise. As it was, he claimed, the charges were so vague that there was little he or anyone else could do to substantiate them. Better still, he advised Morrison to direct his complaints to the State, for the Company had "neither the right to police nor to punish, nor the authority, nor the means of putting a stop to abuses committed by the natives." [13]

Morrison forwarded copies of these letters to Morel in London, who made them available to the British Government and press. The unexpected publication of these missives led Lacourt, who was in Brussels, to interpose "a formal, general and indignant denial" to the "questionable and defamatory allegations of Messrs. Morel, Morrison, Sheppard and other missionaries at Luebo." [14] And, moreover, since Morel published the evangelist's charges and gave voice to his views in Government circles, Lacourt threatened him with legal action. Morel's immediate response was to call upon Morrison to back him up financially and factually, if matters should ever come to court. As Morel was confident that the

Presbyterians would support him, he avowed his complete faith in "the integrity and truthfulness of the American missionaries, whose reports have done so much to move the American Government, and whose duly authorized representative, the Rev. W. M. Morrison, has been frequently received at the White House." [15]

Meanwhile, Morrison was just as resentful of the press campaign inspired by Lacourt which accused him and his associates of "double dealing, lying, hypocrisy . . . and every abomination." [16] Though he was infuriated by Lacourt's flagrant attempt at character assassination, he still remained confident of ultimate victory. In fact, he once again challenged the firm to agree to a searching review of its undertakings. He was so sure that such a probe would vindicate the evangelists that he warned Chaltin that once "the charges are established, we shall endeavour to have you punished, and your agents and all others who are abettors of these wrongs done to the natives." When that day of reckoning came, he made it clear that the C.K. would be compelled to restore the rubber or its value to the people who had been so long exploited.[17]

Both sides sought to strengthen their positions by citing the conclusions of so-called independent observers. The problem was that visitors to the Congo had to depend on missionaries, merchants, or State officers to arrange for lodgings, transportation, and interpreters. This meant that whoever took the traveler in hand was able to a great extent to color the picture he received of conditions in the colony. Itineraries could be planned to suit the purpose of the guide and the words of the people could be interpreted to mean anything the translator desired. As a result, the critics of the Congo administration automatically discounted the reports of witnesses shepherded by the Government, while defenders of the regime denounced the collusive plotting of consuls and evangelists.

Of all the provinces in the Congo, the Kasai was one of the least scrutinized. No foreign diplomat visited the region prior to the arrival of the British vice-consul, Wilfred Thesiger, in 1908. His report, which was submitted to the Foreign Office in September of that year and placed before Parliament the following January, was just what Morrison desired, for it confirmed practically every missionary complaint in language remarkably similar to that used by the evangelists. In graphic detail, Thesiger described how the Company disregarded the best interests of the people so that fields lay fallow, homes were in disrepair, malnutrition was endemic, and everywhere the Kuba were dying from hunger and disease. According to Thesiger, the C.K. had sought to conceal the true nature of its operations by not imposing rubber quotas on the villages near the A.P.C.M. stations. Such deviousness and blatant disregard for human welfare led him to conclude that "no method of reform or change of administration will be of any real benefit to the people of the district unless it includes the entire abolition of this Company." [18]

Even before the Thesiger report was officially communicated to the Belgian Government on January 7, 1909, the substance of the document was known in Brussels. Thus on October 28, 1908, the Government organ, *La Tribune Congolaise,* described the white paper as rubbish and for good measure accused the Presbyterians of being subsidized by Morel and the C.R.A. Nevertheless, the Belgian Colonial Minister (Renkin) and Foreign Minister (Davignon) considered the matter sufficiently serious for them to come to the defense of the beleaguered rubber concern. While Renkin upheld the firm before the Belgian *parlement,* Davignon rebuked the British Government for condoning consular interference in the local administration of the Congo. [19]

Still in all, some benefit did result from Thesiger's tour of the area, for Morrison detected an almost immediate letup in the Company's demands. Apparently orders went out to grant the people sufficient time to plant their crops, build new houses, and spruce up their villages. Despite these improvements, the Presbyterians were not yet ready to lower their guard, for they were aware that Leopold's administrative machinery remained intact and subject to the control of unrepentant officials. Two of these came to see Morrison in Luebo: Munch L. Naur and Hemricourt De Grunne. They were accompanied by Louis Chaltin of the C.K. Though his visitors did not state their real motives, Morrison was not fooled. He divined their intention to carry on an investigation of Sheppard, Thesiger, and himself. Thus when De Grunne asked that Sheppard be permitted to lead him to the same places through which he had guided Thesiger, Morrison refused. Sheppard's time, he explained, was too valuable to be wasted on such a fruitless endeavor.[20]

Since he had done his best to provoke Chaltin, Morrison anticipated being haled into court by the Company. However, he was not sure of when the confrontation would take place and what the basis of the proceedings would be. He decided, therefore, to keep the State Department, the reform associations, and the American consul regularly informed so that they could act on his behalf at a moment's notice. Thus, one of the first messages that William Handley received when he took up his post as consul was one from Morrison declaring that the Presbyterians looked upon him as their defender "if the Company should attempt anything in the way of prosecution of us as a result of any investigation which the State may make of the situation." [21]

When Handley raised the matter with the Attorney General, he was informed that Chaltin intended to initiate an action against Morrison and Sheppard for "having sullied the respectability and injured the credit of the Company by means of certain articles published in the 'Kasai Herald.' " [22] In the complaint, which he filed in February 1909, Chaltin specifically contended that Sheppard's article contained "lying affirmations . . . very damaging to the plaintiff, casting blame on her, tarnishing the honorability of her dealings and injuring her interests." In the absence of a retraction, he demanded 30,000 francs damages from Sheppard. An even greater sum (50,000) was requested of Morrison, for he had expanded on Sheppard's thesis in the series of letters he exchanged with Company and State officials which later found their way into print.[23]

It was hardly a coincidence that the Company waited to press its suit until after Thesiger's damning indictment was made public. For their part, Chaltin and Lacourt were fully convinced that Thesiger was in league with the Presbyterian missionaries, who had housed and guided him, in an invidious plot to deprive Belgium of the Congo. In striking against his clerical allies, they aimed as well at discrediting him, the only course left open to them since his diplomatic immunity precluded his being brought to trial. Actually, through their appeal to the courts for redress, they hoped to be able to undermine public confidence in all their detractors. As it turned out, they played directly into Morrison's hands, for he wanted nothing more than the opportunity to expose the pernicious practices of the smug rubber concern. Both sides, in reality, looked upon the courtroom as a forum wherein they could make an appeal for greater public support.

There can be no denying that the libel trial came just at the right moment, for the reformers desperately needed a *cause celébrè* to regain popular and governmental support. Matters had reached a critical stage in both America and Britain, for it was now much harder to arouse public opinion against Brussels than it had been to foment opposition to Leopold. Each day that passed without the introduction of corrective measures served to strengthen the concessionary concerns, for the public's interest in the reform crusade was waning—so much so, in fact, that Morel despairingly cast about for any means to avoid the "humbug and procrastination" which he believed would result from not pressing the issue.

With the passage of time, it became clear to the reformers that all hope for continued success depended on the support of the American Government. That was the reason why Morel attached so much significance to the libel trial. Regretfully, he confessed to his American colleagues that "nothing is to be hoped for from Germany or France. . . . It is impossible to engineer a movement on the continent . . . like yours and ours. . . . The key . . . is with you." [24] He placed little faith in his own Government, for without the cooperation of France the Liberal cabinet of Asquith seemed unwilling to press Belgium too strongly for fear of straining the *Entente Cordiale*. Morel concluded that the United States was the only power that could apply sufficient pressure to overcome Grey's "insane fear" of Germany. Prior to the libel trial, however, there seemed to be little likelihood that Washington would take any action, for there was considerable official disenchantment with the reformers who had too often plagued the bureaucrats.

As far as Morrison was concerned, the impending court contest was a flagrant example of legal harassment and warranted the State

Department's intervention. He even made a special point of reminding Handley of his obligation as consul to protect American citizens who had been unjustly accused.[25] And, since the Congo Reform Association concluded that the United States Government was not likely to take the initiative unless provoked to action by the libel case, everything possible was done to exploit the affair. One of the leaders of the organization, John Daniels, expressed his hope that the trial would "give the Department of State a happy opportunity to intervene in the general situation." [26]

Given these circumstances, Morel urgently counseled his American associates to do everything possible to persuade President Taft to consider the Morrison prosecution as an unfriendly act or, failing that, as "ample justification for American consular jurisdiction." [27] Three years earlier, he had attempted to exploit the conviction of Edgar Stannard of the Congo Balolo Mission on a charge of defamation to induce the interposition of the British Government. Although Stannard did receive legal assistance from the British consul, he nevertheless thwarted the reformers by choosing to return home rather than to remain to continue the uneven struggle. What is more, the Free State upheld his appeal so as to avoid giving the British a reason to intervene. The trial of Morrison and Sheppard afforded Morel a second opportunity to employ the same strategy. In both cases, his object was to get the government of the accused to insist upon consular jurisdiction. Morrison did his part by questioning the competence of a Congo court to try Americans.

When news of the Company's legal maneuver reached the United States, the Southern Presbyterian Church reacted quickly in order to protect the interests of its ministers. Chester almost immediately contacted the Department of State to complain that the trial date (May 25, 1909) and the location (Leopoldville) greatly disadvantaged the accused. At the very minimum, he demanded that Handley be ordered to attend the hearing to insure compliance with international standards of justice.[28] Because Secretary of State Philander C. Knox did not acknowledge his letter,[29] Chester decided to go to Washington to get direct action. By using all of his political leverage, he managed to secure an interview with the recently installed head of the State Department. Since Chester's appraisal of the situation was confirmed by Handley's dispatches, Knox instructed the American legation in Brussels to seek a delay of the trial and a change of venue.[30]

To make sure that Washington did not forget about the trial, the Congo Reform Association and the Southern Presbyterian Church organized nationwide protest meetings. After each gathering, "letters and resolutions from all sorts of religious associations" poured in petitioning the Government "to see that justice and [a] fair trial is obtained for those missionaries." [31] Each denomination stated its membership so that the administration would be aware of its political strength and not treat its views lightly.[32]

One of the more important groups to consider the issue was the Council of the Alliance of Reformed Churches which met in New York in June 1909. Like most other clerics, the Council delegates feared that the gagging of the evangelists might be a dangerous precedent. Therefore, at the urging of Robert Whyte, the churchmen importuned

> the President of the United States to insist upon the observance of the Berlin and Brussels Acts and the provisions of the treaty between the American Government and the Congo Independent State so far as the interests of these missionaries are concerned, and protests for justice.[33]

A six-man committee, which included Dr. Chester and Elihu Root, was appointed to convey the appeal of the Convention to President Taft. Root neither solicited nor desired a position on the committee and was ignorant of the responsibility assigned to him until he was informed of it by an apologetic Chester. Though Root politely declined to serve because of his former connection with the Government, he did agree to ask Knox to "give this matter . . . attention and see whether the Department can appropriately take any action in the case." [34]

In the end, the Presbyterian committee had to be satisfied with meeting Taft's private secretary, who sent them home with his assurance that their petition would be brought to the President's attention. Others who contacted the President included: Governor Curtis Guild, Jr., of Massachusetts; the Reverend Herbert S.

Johnson, who was a nephew of Senator Crane of the Bay State; John Marshall Harlan (on behalf of Sheppard's mother); and Senator Joseph F. Johnston of Alabama (as a service to James Rutherford Lapsley). President Taft was quick to perceive the need to appease the Protestant Republican establishment, for he instructed Knox to raise the issue at the next cabinet meeting so that they could determine the best means of upholding the interests of the evangelists. Following the discussion of the matter, directions were sent to Wilson in Brussels to inform the Belgian Government that the United States viewed the trial with "acute interest and no little concern." Furthermore, he was to make it clear that the fairness of the proceedings would be considered as a barometer of Belgium's reform intentions. He was even to go so far as to hint that American diplomatic recognition might depend on the outcome of the litigation.[35] At the same time, Handley was ordered to attend the trial to render whatever assistance might be needed.

Though he was prepared to do everything possible to preserve Morrison's and Sheppard's freedom and to prevent a miscarriage of justice, Knox failed to see how he could question the authority of the Congo judiciary to hear the case. His own legal experts advised him that extraterritorial consular jurisdiction could be claimed only on the basis of treaty right. Morrison and Morel were understandably disappointed when the Solicitor General ruled that Congolese courts could try American citizens even if the United States did not recognize the Government, for the annexation was the result of a legal compact between two sovereign nations.[36]

Because the case was to be argued in Leopoldville, the defendants and their Kuba witnesses had to undertake a long, arduous trip downriver. Since boats were not able to approach too close to Luebo during the dry season, it was difficult to arrange transportation. Nevertheless, Handley opposed any plan to transfer the trial to Lusambo, for Leopoldville was much more accessible to him. But while he made it to the courtroom on the appointed day, the defendants did not. They explained that after their ship had run aground for a second time, the captain had refused to endanger further either the vessel or the passengers by continuing the voyage to Leopoldville.[37] To avoid the case being lost by default, Handley petitioned the presiding magistrate, Charles Louis Gianpetri, to delay the trial. The judge obliged the consul by putting off the proceedings until July 30, 1909. Chaltin posed no objection to the deferment because he wished to be present when the Belgian Colonial Secretary toured the Kasai on his scheduled inspection tour.

Though they did not forfeit their case, Morrison and Sheppard did have to pay a price for their tardiness, for they lost the corroborative testimony of Thesiger, who could not postpone his departure a second time. When the court ruled his absentee affidavit inadmissible, the evangelists feared that they would be forced to depend on the depositions of the Kuba.[38] Such a prospect was not very encouraging, for the courts attached little weight to the words of African witnesses who often became confused and frightened and said anything they thought would please the State.

Because they had resigned themselves to the prospect of being convicted, Morrison and Sheppard had made little effort to seek legal aid. They planned simply to state the facts as they understood them and to describe all that they had seen. In the event that the court should rule against them, they intended to refuse to pay any fine and thus dramatize their case by going off to prison.[39] Only the realization that the fate of the other Protestant missions was bound up in theirs induced them to agree to be represented by counsel. By the time they recognized that truth, however, the Compagnie du Kasai had secured the services of the only independent attorney available. Handley's last-minute application to the Government for permission to employ a law clerk attached to the staff of the Director of Justice was rejected by the Governor-General on the ground that it was contrary to regulations to assign public servants to serve private interests. The truth, of course, was that the Government was unwilling to assist the missionaries whose defense was based very largely on a condemnation of its activities.

Since they were compelled to seek legal help from without, Handley advised the Southern Presbyterians to authorize their representative in Britain to engage a bilingual Belgian advocate who was familiar with the Congo situation. Though he had departed from the scene, Thesiger evinced his concern by cooperating in the search for a qualified lawyer. In the end, like most things, the matter was turned over to Morel. He promptly contacted the Belgian socialist leader, Emile Vandervelde, to ask "if Americans accept responsibility for expenses could you put me in touch with honest young Belgian lawyer to defend Morrison in Congo against Kasai Company at Leopoldville." [40] Vandervelde immediately volunteered to accept the case, if there were no objection to him. On the contrary, the missionaries were quite willing to be defended by the agnostic politician. So that their counsel (who was not yet identified) might have enough time to be present for the trial, Gianpetri agreed to another postponement, thus setting back the proceedings until September 24, 1909. This second expression of his fairness led Handley to hope that an impartial trial might be possible after all.

Though Vandervelde had considerable political experience and some personal knowledge of the Congo, he had never appeared before the bar. He could scarcely have chosen a more controversial case in which to make his debut. Some Belgian newspapers went so far as to accuse him of treason for undertaking the defense of the foreign clerics against his own nationals. He insisted, however, that justice did not recognize foreigners and that he was simply continuing in the Congo the fight for reform that he had waged at home. In interviews, he made it clear that his acceptance of the case was dictated primarily by his concern for the welfare of the oppressed Congolese rather than by any preference for the Protestant clergymen. As much as he might try to play the role of the selfless humanitarian, Vandervelde remained a politician who was acutely aware that the trial gave him an opportunity to embarrass the Catholic party then ruling Belgium. To Chaltin, Vandervelde's presence was additional proof that there was a conspiracy between the American missionaries, the Belgian socialists, and the British consuls in order to compel Belgium to abandon the colony to Britain. And if it were at all possible, he intended to demonstrate his conviction in court.

After many maneuvers and much delay, the trial finally commenced on September 20th, "in a large room of planks set upon pedestals of brick; the walls . . . roughly painted in green; the

many windows . . . minus panes." [41] There were two clear group-
ings in the courtroom: on one side sat the Protestant missionaries
and foreign consuls and their partisans, while across the room sat
the Catholic evangelists and representatives of the Company and
the State. The Reverend T. Hope Morgan expressed the fear of the
large Protestant delegation that if the case were lost it would be a
severe blow for the whole reform movement.[42] According to Thesiger, all that the C.K. really wanted was an initial conviction so that
it could flood the world's press with the story of its vindication.

The course of the proceedings was determined almost immediately when Gianpetri dismissed the case against Morrison on a
technicality. The plaintiffs had intended to institute two separate
but related suits: one against Sheppard for writing the article in
question, and the other against Morrison for casting aspersions on
the Company's reputation in his published correspondence. Mistakenly, however, the court clerk combined the two summonses so
that Morrison was accused only of being the editor of the journal
which had published the offensive article. In the opinion of the
court the libelants were remiss in not detecting the error and
instituting supplemental proceedings. Because of their failure to do
so, Gianpetri excused Morrison as a defendant in the trial.[43] If the
decision had been left up to him, Morrison would have opposed
this move, for it meant that the hearing would be concerned only
with the general indictment in Sheppard's article rather than with
his specific charges against the Compagnie du Kasai.

In some respects the trial resembled the theater of the absurd,
for an agnostic pleaded for the missionaries, while a socialist spoke
for the capitalists. Gaston Vandermeeren, who was Vandervelde's
associate in *le parti ouvrier belge,* tried to prove that Sheppard's
article referred to the Kasai Company, that its publication was a
cause of serious moral and material injury, and that it had been
maliciously motivated in an attempt to frustrate Belgium's annexation of the Congo. In essence, he repeated Chaltin's charge that "in
using the words 'chartered companies,' Dr. Sheppard certainly
aims at the Company Kasai, since being on the spot he knows that
there is no other company gathering rubber in that section, and it
is impossible for him to aim at another company since it has been

made known everywhere by certain articles that have been written reproaching the State for having given the Kasai Company the monopoly of the rubber trade in the Kasai District." [44]

If Sheppard had not been hostile in his attitude, Vandermeeren claimed that he would have communicated the reasons for his displeasure to Company officials before making public his criticisms of the firm's operations. He did not do so, the Company attorney charged, because his article and Thesiger's report were intended as dual salvoes in the propaganda barrage laid down by Morel to prevent Belgium from gaining control of the Congo. It was Vandermeeren's contention that Morrison had invited Thesiger to the Kasai at the urging of Morel to discredit the C.K. and undermine its operations so that Belgium would find it financially unprofitable to retain control of the colony. [45] Though there was some basis of truth in this assertion, Vandervelde was able to refute the broader lie.

When finally he got his chance, Vandervelde, most spectators agreed, "made a magnificent defense—his speech was a marvel of eloquence, invincible logic, burning sarcasm and pethetia [*sic*] appeal for justice to be done." [46] He emphasized how ridiculous it was to conclude that Sheppard would seriously endeavor to forestall Belgium from annexing the Congo by means of a vague article in an obscure journal addressed primarily to Southern Presbyterians. [47] If it meant anything at all, Vandervelde maintained that Sheppard's revelation of abuses had indicated the need for a change in administration and did not of itself entail opposition to Belgium's assumption of sovereignty. If the evangelist had really intended to stimulate resistance to such a move, Vandervelde claimed, the tract would have been less general and much more highly publicized. Rather than being a first shot in a subversive campaign to deliver the Congo to Britain as Vandermeeren had asserted, the article was described by Vandervelde as a humanitarian appeal made in an attempt to arouse concern for the people of the Kasai. In reality, Sheppard's purpose was neither as innocent as Vandervelde pretended nor as devious as Vandermeeren imagined. While he may not have opposed Belgium's right to the Congo, he did protest any continuation of the practices of the Compagnie du Kasai. His article was intended to attract both financial aid for the mission and moral support for his effort to help the Kuba.

Vandermeeren's repeated appeals to patriotic and religious prejudice seriously disturbed the evangelists and their counsel. They were angered by his snide reminders that the Catholics never observed any of the evils so vividly described by the Protestants. Even more galling was his suggestion that their protests were caused by their jealousy of the State's supposed favoritism of the Catholics. What he really wanted the court to believe was that the Presbyterian clerics were agents of an alien power who had lied for base ends. With much heat, but less candor, Vandervelde retorted that the Protestant missionaries respected the Catholics and wanted only to be treated equally. Furthermore, he demanded that the plaintiffs produce conclusive proof to substantiate their allegation that there was collusion between the American missionaries and the British consul designed to effect Britain's seizure of the colony. When Vandermeeren admitted that he lacked such documentation, Vandervelde explained that it was because the C.K. had fabricated the conspiracy in order to save its reputation.[48]

Whereas Vandermeeren was chiefly interested in exploiting the trial to silence the consuls and evangelists, Vandervelde's major purpose was to get the court to condemn the policies and practices of the Compagnie du Kasai. In order to gain permission to introduce testimony which could corroborate Morrison's and Sheppard's complaints, Vandervelde offered to acknowledge the possibility that the C.K. had been harmed by the article though he, himself, did not believe that to be the case. Vandermeeren opposed the motion, for he feared that the trial might degenerate into an inquest of the Company procedures. The basis of his objection was that the Congolese code "made no mention of the right of proof and therefore in point of law the truth or otherwise of the assertions had no bearing on the case." Moreover, he reminded the court that only private individuals and not the Company itself had been mentioned by name in the article.[49] Vandervelde declared that by refusing to allow the Kuba to testify, the Company was admitting its guilt. Since no proof had been presented to show that the article had caused the Company injury or that Sheppard had any spiteful intent in writing it, Vandervelde moved that the suit be dismissed.[50]

In the end, when all extraneous issues were stripped away, the core of the case was reduced to the question of whether the following assertion: "there are armed sentries of chartered trading companies who force the men and women to spend most of their nights making rubber, and the price they receive for it is so meagre that they cannot live upon it" was false, libelous, or harmful in any way to the Compagnie du Kasai. After due deliberation, Judge Gianpetri ruled that:

a) The defendant Sheppard . . . did not have a malicious intention of injuring the Kasai Company by publishing the abuses imputed to the subordinates of said company.

b) That the defendant Sheppard likewise had no intention of laying the blame on the company, or challenging the honesty of its acts or injuring its credit.

c) That the defendant Sheppard did not intend to make an attack on the said company, to which he attributed no responsibility for the abusive acts of its subordinates.

d) That . . . the article did not and could not refer to the Kasai Company which was held entirely disconnected with the abuses denounced.[51]

Inasmuch as Vandermeeren had failed to demonstrate that Sheppard's article had caused the C.K. serious moral or material injury entitling it to compensation, Gianpetri dismissed the suit and ordered the plaintiff to pay forty-two francs for court costs.

Both sides, as it turned out, were dissatisfied with the decision, which bore all the earmarks of a *jugement d'expédient*. While it was true that the evangelists were acquitted, it was accomplished in such a way as to minimize the damage to the Company's reputation. Lacourt and Chaltin lost the case only because they were unable to sustain their own assertions, not because anything had been proved against them. And Sheppard was exonerated only because Vandervelde demonstrated that the missionary had directly criticized only armed sentries who were not parties to the suit and not the Compagnie du Kasai. This allowed Gianpetri to conclude that the article was nothing more than an appeal to American philanthropists for money to promote the A.P.C.M.'s work and thereby to frustrate the mission's desire for an inquiry into conditions in the Kasai. Vandervelde took the line he did so as to secure an acquittal for Sheppard and deny the rubber firm the opportunity of exploiting a legal victory. At least one outsider thought that the evangelists had "run away from their charges against the Company and [had] not covered themselves with glory." [52] But this strategy was adopted only after Morrison was denied the opportunity of presenting his specific indictment against the offending concern.

In some ways, the trial appeared to be a play in which everyone acted out his role fully aware of what the conclusion would be. However, it seems that the ending was rewritten some time between the time the suit was initiated and the verdict delivered. In all likelihood, the integrity of the presiding magistrate and the active interest of the American Government accounted for the revision of the script. At least Morrison inclined toward this view when he thanked Knox for his manifest aid in securing an acquittal.[53] American displeasure over the proceedings was made apparent by a hardening of Washington's line on all issues relating to the Congo. Brussels was particularly dismayed by the State Department's efforts to connect the case with labor and tax matters. In response to this pressure, Belgium agreed to exempt the African employees of the A.P.C.M. from assessed and personal taxes.[54] In a further effort to satisfy American protests, the Belgian Government hinted that it would act favorably on future Protestant applications for new mission sites if the evangelists would promise to "observe the law and respect the public authorities of the country whose hospitality they enjoy." [55] It is not out of the question that a similar *quid pro quo* determined the outcome of the trial. At the very minimum, Wilson's strictures and Handley's admonitions guaranteed a fair trial.[56]

By itself, the verdict did not threaten the end of the rubber system. But in the wake of the trial a score of Government officials rushed to the Kasai to look into conditions there. As a result of their investigation, Renkin was moved to strip the Compagnie du Kasai of its extralegal monopoly and to order the restoration of competitive trade as part of his broader program of reform.[57] Following these changes, the pressure to gather rubber was relaxed, and the lot of the people noticeably improved. Even the Compagnie du Kasai ultimately thrived under the new system, for the discovery of diamonds in the region assured its prosperity just when the rubber supply was diminishing.

Most of the credit for the amelioration of conditions in the Kasai must unquestionably go to the Presbyterian evangelists. They were courageous, resourceful, and unrelenting crusaders for justice and decency in the Congo. As a result of their commitment to reform, they became embroiled in many disputes. In this connection, the libel trial was a tempest of more than ordinary significance. It galvanized the reformers and gave them something to focus on at a critical moment. More than that, it induced the United States to take a more direct hand in the effort to root out the last vestiges of the "Leopoldian system."

NOTES

1. Vinson, p. 77.
2. *Ibid.*, p. 75.
3. *Official Organ of the Congo Reform Association*, August 1907, p. 32. Hereafter cited as *O.O.C.R.A.* This letter from an A.P.C.M. member was written to Morel on May 31, 1907.
4. Morrison diary, March 7, 1899.
5. *Ibid.*, March 28, 1899.
6. Rochester to Chester, December 18, 1907, enclosed in Numerical File, 1906–1910, Cases 1806/80–1806/205, No. 192. Hereafter cited as S.D. 192.
7. A Belgian judge, Edmond Janssens, an Italian judge in the service of the Free State, Baron Nisco, and a Swiss justice, Edmond De Schumacher.
8. V. Lacourt, *A Propos Du Congo* (Brussels, 1908), pp. 35–38.
9. Vass to Morel, July 22, 1908, M.P.
10. *Kasai Herald* (January 1, 1908), pp. 12–13.
11. Thurstan to Grey, April 20, 1911, F.O. 403/425.
12. *O.O.C.R.A.*, June 1908, p. 19. Dreypondt to Morrison, March 6, 1908.
13. *Great Britain Foreign Office: Africa, 1909, No. 1, Cd. 4466*, p. 42, the Thesiger Report.
14. *O.O.C.R.A.*, June 1908, p. 23. Lacourt to Morel, June 13, 1908.
15. *Ibid.*, Morel to Lacourt, June 15, 1908.
16. Morel to Morrison, July 7, 1908, M.P.
17. *Cd. 4466*, pp. 43–44. Morrison to Chaltin, August 18, 1908.
18. *Ibid.*, pp. 6–7.

19. Davignon to Hardinge, January 23, 1909, *Documents Diplomatiques,* p. 23. According to Arthur Hardinge, the British Minister to Belgium, the Thesiger Report was not viewed as being impartial in Brussels, for most of the information came from Protestant missionaries "whose sentiments towards the State were notorious." See Hardinge to Grey, February 4, 1909, F.O. 403/409.

20. Morrison to De Grunne, October 9, 1908, enclosed in Numerical File, 1906–1910, Cases 1806/461–1806/580, No. 195. Hereafter cited as S.D. 195.

21. Morrison to American Consul-General Boma, October 6, 1908, enclosed in Handley to State Department, December 4, 1908, Numerical File, 1906–1910, Cases 12024–12053/60, No. 792. Hereafter cited as S.D. 792. Handley was appointed to the post on June 22, 1908.

22. Handley to State Department, February 26, 1909, S.D. 792.

23. Vinson, pp. 90–91.

24. Slade, p. 333, n. 3, quotes Morel to Daniels, 15 IV 09. Morel feared that if Britain and the United States waited for the Belgian Colonial Minister to tour the Congo and then return and suggest reforms it would be like "two years of . . . treading water," which was why he was so anxious for Washington to give a push to Whitehall. See Morel to Daniels, March 12, 1909, M.P.

25. Morrison to Handley, February 24, 1909, S.D. 792.

26. Daniels to Huntington Wilson, May 11, 1909, State Department Numerical File, 1906–1910, Cases 12053/61–12074, No. 793. Hereafter cited as S.D. 793.

27. Daniels to Root, May 22, 1909, encloses Morel to Daniels, March 12, 1909, and Morel to Barbour, May 13, 1909, Root Papers, Library of Congress, Box 59.

28. Chester to Knox, April 13, 1909, S.D. 792. Chester initially presented the case to Robert Bacon, who was Acting Secretary, in February 1909.

29. The American envoy in Belgium, Henry Lane Wilson, was of the view that "Mr. Knox felt a little less strongly than Mr. Root about Congo misgovernment and was less amenable to missionary pressure." Hardinge to Grey, May 17, 1909, F.O. 403/409.

30. Authorities in Brussels responded that they had no jurisdiction in the case and thus any appeal for a postponement had to be initiated by the parties concerned.

31. M. H. to Huntington Wilson, July 2, 1909, S.D. 793.

32. Among the religious bodies which applied pressure on the Government were:
    (1) The General Assembly of the Presbyterian Church in the United States;
    (2) Board of Missions, Methodist Episcopal Church South;
    (3) American Friends Board of Foreign Missions;
    (4) Federal Council of the Churches of Christ of America;
    (5) Board of Foreign Missions of the Reformed Churches in America;
    (6) General Conference of Free Baptists;
    (7) The Domestic and Foreign Missionary Society of the Protestant Episcopal Church;
    (8) Board of Missions of the General Synod of the Evangelical Lutheran Church in the United States of America;
    (9) Free Methodist Church of North America;
    (10) The Executive Committee of Foreign Missions of the Presbyterian Church in the United States of America.
See S.D. 793.

33. *The Missionary* (August 1909), p. 393. The resolution passed on June 24, 1909.

34. Root to Knox, June 26, 1909, S.D. 793. Root was then a Senator.

35. State Department to H. L. Wilson, July 2, 1909, S.D. 793.

36. Scott to Clark, August 7, 1909, S.D. 793. Alvey Adee later commented that the United States could no more judge Belgium's right to annex the Congo than Belgium had the right to decide America's title to Alaska or Hawaii.

37. Morrison to Handley, May 26, 1909, enclosed in Handley to the State Department, June 14, 1909, S.D. 793. Morrison claimed to have fired the captain for refusing to continue the voyage, but he was not discharged until 1915.

38. In a memorandum prepared for Grey upon his return, Thesiger urged that if, among other things, Belgium did not guarantee equal freedom for all religious missions then a claim of consular jurisdiction should be weighed.

39. John Holt, a leading Liverpool merchant and a staunch ally of Morel, expressed the extreme sentiment that if the "prosecution of Morrison will make the United States do something terrible I hope Morrison may be put into prison if not executed, much as I desire his freedom and life to be respected. We want the U.S.A. to act strongly." Holt to Morel, n.d., M.P.

40. Morel to Vandervelde, July 3/6, 1909, M.P.

41. *O.O.C.R.A.*, January 1910, pp. 462–463.

42. Morgan to Chester, May 28, 1909, M.P. Thesiger similarly advised Grey that it was "impossible to over-estimate the importance of the trial," for it represented "an attempt on the part of the State to destroy . . . the power of the Missionary Societies to criticize the maladministration of the State and the Companies in which it holds a majority of the shares." Thesiger to Grey, March 12, 1909, F.O. 403/409.

43. Handley to the State Department, October 19, 1909, S.D. 793. Gianpetri said that his decision was based more on Congo ordinances than the Belgian press law which held that "when the author of [an] article complained against is judicially known, the publisher is not responsible and should be eliminated from the suit."

44. Vinson, pp. 90–91.

45. *O.O.C.R.A.*, January 1910, p. 464.

46. Morrison to Morel, September 22, 1909, M.P.

47. Morrison, however, had made copies of the article available to leading Company and State officials.

48. *O.O.C.R.A.*, January 1910, p. 465.

49. Armstrong to Grey, September 27, 1909, F.O. 403/410. According to Thurstan, the applicable principle of the Code Napoleon was: "the greater the truth the greater the libel." All that mattered was whether injury had been suffered and the intent had been malicious. It was not enough to plead as one could in an English or American court that the statement was true and made in good faith in the public interest. See Thurstan to Tilley, September 25, 1909, F.O. 367/167.

50. Handley to the State Department, September 21, 1909, S.D. 793.

51. Gianpetri's decision, pp. 13–14, enclosed in Handley to the State Department, October 19, 1909, S.D. 793.

52. Minute of Walter Langley, November 29, 1909, F.O. 367/168.

53. Morrison to Knox, December 15, 1909, S.D. 793. Britain had also increased her pressure upon Belgium at this time, leading Renkin to promise far-reaching reforms on October 5, 1909.

54. *The Missionary* (October 1909), p. 490. The exemption was to become effective on July 1, 1909.

55. *Ibid.* (August 1909), p. 393.

56. Handley told his British counterpart that the "American Government intended taking energetic action whatever the decision in the case—that they will in fact protest strongly, if the Kasai Company lose, on the ground that the Belgian Government should never have allowed the case to come into the courts at all,

and if the Kasai Company win, on the ground that injustice is being done to American citizens." Thurstan to Tilley, September 25, 1909, F.O. 367/167.

57. The Company filed suit to protect its economic interests and the Government retaliated with a substantial countersuit. The case ultimately was settled out of court on February 11, 1911. The State had to give up its stock in the concern and its power to appoint supervisory personnel. In return, the C.K. had to compensate the Government for its financial sacrifice and acknowledge the loss of the privileges granted to it by King Leopold.

8

Conflict over the *Chefferie* System
and Domestic Slavery

The satisfactory conclusion of the libel trial did not resolve all of the mission's difficulties. One of the major problems still outstanding involved the Government's tacit acceptance of domestic slavery and the mission's unyielding opposition to that institution. While the State showed every intention of suppressing the slave trade, it was not prepared to interfere with domestic bondage. The main reason was that such an effort would have occasioned general and violent resistance beyond the power of the Government to control. Since the administration could neither abolish nor approve of domestic slavery, it simply pretended that the practice did not exist. Administrators who sanctioned the return of fugitives to their masters claimed only to be upholding the authority of indigenous leaders.

Because the Presbyterians welcomed the runaways and allowed them to settle on or near their stations, Luebo became a magnet attracting escaped bondsmen. But, since slaves were considered investments in the Congo, and added to the power and prestige of their owners, most masters were understandably reluctant to recognize the freedom of the fugitives and demanded the return of their property. The willingness of the A.P.C.M. to afford sanctuary to even a small number of escapees plunged the evangelists into countless palavers with local chiefs and Government officials. Not surprisingly, because they protected an outcast rabble, the Presbyterians were always at a disadvantage in these disputes. In their zeal for social justice, they not only alienated the local tribal chiefs but as well placed the mission in jeopardy, and thus Luebo became an "island shut around in peculiar isolation."[1]

To say the least, it was ironical that a Southern mission should get into trouble for, of all things, trying to stamp out slavery. But,

as early as June 1894, Captain Pelzer rebuked Snyder for liberat-
ing slaves without a license. When Adamson asked him how this
was possible, considering the fact that the State contended that
domestic servitude did not exist, he replied that he was enforcing a
regulation prohibiting flight from one tribe to another. Not long
afterward, the missionaries succeeded in securing a fixed price
redemption law as a reward for nursing an ailing official back to
good health. Accordingly, owners were now compelled to accept
eight pieces of cloth for each slave that they possessed who wished
to be free. Shortly thereafter, however, the cooperative officer was
recalled and his successor nullified the regulation at the behest of
Chief Zappo. As a result, the Presbyterians tried to restrict themselves simply to teaching the evils of slavery, but that proved
nearly impossible.

In an effort to consolidate his control of the unsettled colony
and to prevent emigration to unpacified districts, Leopold, in
October 1891, divided the Congo into *chefferies* which were to be
administered by native rulers subject to European supervision.
Subsequently, the system was formalized by a series of decrees
promulgated in 1906. Under these regulations, a *chefferie* might
consist of either one village or several governed by a chief who had
been confirmed in that position by the State. Usually, hereditary
leaders were appointed, unless they were demonstrably incapable
or corrupt. Once a person was assigned to a *chefferie,* he was not
supposed to leave it without the express approval of his chief.
Anyone departing without permission or a contract of employment
might be arrested by the State and repatriated.

Belgium perpetuated the system but placed more emphasis on
civilizing the people. It was the intention of the new administration
to apply the policy in areas of the Congo where it had not been
introduced previously. But every effort to implement it at Luebo
was resisted by the missionaries. Though the evangelists claimed to
support the *chefferie* in the abstract, they did everything possible to
thwart its realization at Luebo. It was not the principle to which
they objected, but the manner in which it was put into practice.
The Presbyterians were firmly convinced that the State was much
more interested in exploiting the colony at the least possible cost

than it was in preserving traditional authority. Furthermore, they believed that the *chefferie* system was nothing more than a cover to conceal a fugitive slave hunt which was intended to transfer to Luluabourg the men who worked for the A.P.C.M. at Luebo. Official explanations declaring that the move was designed to reconstitute fragmented tribes and to restore vagabonds to their place of origin were rejected by the evangelists who claimed that in reality their former adherents were bound over to alien chiefs who were tools of the administration.[2]

One of the most serious disputes arising from this controversy involved Morrison and Hemricourt De Grunne, a young Belgian nobleman who became *chef de secteur de Luluabourg* not long after his arrival in the Kasai in 1906. At first, he was well received by the Protestant evangelists. Motte Martin considered him "just and fair" even though he was a Roman Catholic.[3] But relations between the officer and mission deteriorated after Morrison accused him of commanding an expedition to corral slaves under the pretence of returning fugitives to their *chefferies*. In return De Grunne criticized the Presbyterians for falsely leading the people to believe that they could purchase their freedom for sixteen pieces of cloth. A much more serious matter, he contended, was their encouragement of insubordination and lawlessness, particularly as they invited slackers and troublemakers to settle in Luebo. His effort to remove such shirkers, he maintained, was only intended to restore order in the area.

The matter might have been forgotten after this initial acrimonious exchange, if Lachlan Vass had not sent a photo to Morel showing thirty Congolese captives being led away with ropes about their necks. Following Morel's exploitation of the incident, De Grunne was harshly taken to task in the British press and even in some Belgian papers for impressing workers and disrupting mission activities. Because he was outraged by what he insisted was the unwarranted tarring of his good name, De Grunne demanded that Morrison acknowledge the falsity of the charges and help him to rehabilitate his reputation. But the most that the evangelist would concede was that De Grunne might have been taken advantage of by shrewd slave owners. This did not mollify the bitter officer who ordered Munch L. Naur to proceed to Luebo in October 1908 to investigate the affair. In response to that magistrate's questions, all that Morrison would admit was that a number of people, who were ignorant of the *chefferie* law, had been brutally arrested by De Grunne. Although he could not prove it, he contended that some of the Luba who had been seized were being forced to work for the State.

De Grunne's intention of filing suit against Morrison was so well-known in the Kasai that *La Tribune Congolaise* prematurely reported on November 5, 1908, that he had already started proceedings against the evangelist for defamation of character. Chester called the clipping to the attention of Root, but the Secretary of State refused to take any action solely on the basis of a newspaper account. His caution was warranted, for De Grunne apparently decided to wait until after the Compagnie du Kasai had finished with the missionaries.

De Grunne did not lack for defenders. Jules Renkin, for one, went out of his way to praise his character and performance. The Colonial Secretary fully supported his explanation that he had done nothing more than return some vagabond Congolese to their rightful *chefferie*. At the same time, Renkin made clear his contempt for anyone who would malign the reputation of an officer serving in the Congo, especially when it took two months for the aggrieved party to hear of the smear and then an additional sixty days for him to make his side of the case known to the public in Europe. Morrison, he prophesied, would be compelled to eat his own words. Acting independently, Count François De Grunne won the support of Arthur Hardinge in his battle "to vindicate by every means in his power, his son's honour and that of his family against the reckless slanders of the American missionaries." [4]

Normal relations between the mission and the local administration had not yet been restored when Morrison once again attacked De Grunne. This time he accused him of imperiling the A.P.C.M. by informing the Kuba monarch, Kot aPe, that Sheppard had charged him with being responsible for the murder of several slaves at the recent interment of his sister. As a result, Morrison feared that the *Lukenga* might be tempted to attack the mission with the covert encouragement of the State. In reality, the *chef de secteur* had visited the king only in order to find out more about Thesiger's inspection tour.[5] Moreover, when he learned of the evangelist's fears of a possible Kuba rebellion, he sent an urgent message to the Hungarian ethnographer Emil Torday at Mushenge asking him for his assessment of the situation "so that I may take at once all necessary precautions." [6] If Torday thought it desirable, he was prepared to send immediate relief. The explorer replied that there was not a shadow of truth to the report. According to him, "it was just an incident of the campaign of calumny which had been carried on for years against the Nyimi." As a matter of fact, he considered it comparable to the despicable allegation that Kot aPe was to blame for the bloodbath at his sister's funeral.[7]

To give him credit, De Grunne actually tried to verify Sheppard's charges against the Kuba sovereign. He even went so far as to take Kot aPe into custody in an effort to determine who really was to blame for the massacre of the slaves. In the end, the investigation proved fruitless, for not a single Kuba witness was prepared to testify against his monarch. Kot aPe himself disclaimed any responsibility for the traditional killing of the chattels, but he did agree, under pressure, to hand over the guilty parties to the State.

Either the Presbyterians were more resolute than most or just more foolhardy, for not even the reality of one lawsuit and the distinct possibility of another were enough to induce them to proceed cautiously. Thus, on the very eve of the libel trial, Morrison did not hesitate to send Dr. L. J. Coppedge to investigate the validity of reports that gross outrages were being perpetrated in the region between Luebo and Luluabourg. In short order, Coppedge discovered clear indications of pillage, arson, and rape. Most of the violence was traced to the efforts of the *chef de poste de Luluabourg* to recruit workers for the Great Lakes Railroad while at the same time replacing uncooperative native authorities with supporters of a chief (Kalamba's son) whose favor the State was trying to win. While the objectives of sub-lieutenant M. Kervyn de Meerendré might have been within the law, his excessively brutal methods were not.

Morrison declared that if the State were truly interested in upholding law and order and establishing good relations with the A.P.C.M., then the *commissaire de district* must severely punish Kervyn. Since he really did not expect him to do so, he sent a full transcript of the evidence to Morel and Arthur Conan Doyle, to be used as ammunition to forestall Anglo-American recognition of Belgian rule in the Congo. Simultaneously, he prevailed upon the Protestant clerics who had convened in Kinshasa in September 1909 to pass a resolution condemning compulsory labor. But just to be on the safe side for once, he asked that the resolve should not be made public until after the libel trial so as not to prejudice the outcome of the proceedings.

As if he were playing an old part, Renkin once again took it upon himself to rebut Morrison before the Belgian *parlement*. First of all, he wondered why the evangelist had not personally informed him of Kervyn's alleged misconduct when they had both been in Boma during August. Why, he asked, did Morrison entrust the information to Père Emeri Cambier who was on his way home to Belgium for a rest? Though he promised a searching investigation of Coppedge's charges, he was satisfied that the indictment would be found to be as false as the one brought against De Grunne.[8]

In a letter to the *London Times* challenging Renkin's assertions, Morrison claimed to have transmitted a detailed report of the incident to the State on July 13, 1909. If he had failed to meet the Colonial Secretary, he explained, it was not out of design, but only because he was preoccupied with the libel trial.[9] Besides he really did not trust the Government, for, as he informed Morel: "The fact is that the Commissaire himself is into it, for it was he who sent these people, caught, down on the State Steamer in August to be transshipped to the Upper Congo somewhere."[10]

As it turned out, not even the acquittal of Sheppard ended the legal harassment of the mission, for, just a few months after the favorable verdict had been rendered, the touring magistrate, Val Gelders, arrived in Luebo to secure depositions from the evangelists for some unexplained purpose. Morrison was quite disturbed, for he was convinced that the "rascals" were scraping the countryside with a fine-tooth comb hoping to come up with something with which to muzzle the mission.[11] Because he anticipated further legal action, he renewed his appeal to Handley for protection. The American consul shared his apprehension, for it seemed to him that the Company and De Grunne had "set Lukengu on the mission" with the intent of intimidating its members.[12] To make matters worse for the evangelists, Thurstan reported that De Grunne and Kervyn could think of nothing else but of gaining revenge. Both Handley and Thurstan concluded that the Belgian Government had "determined on a policy of repression . . . with respect to these missionaries."[13] To prevent any harm from coming to the evangelists, the consuls quickly brought the matter to the attention of the Vice-Governor-General.

Finally, on June 17, 1910, after two years of conflict and tension, Morrison and De Grunne agreed upon a formula to settle their dispute. At the suggestion of Thurstan, they exchanged letters in which each stated his own version of what had taken place, in a manner satisfactory to the other. Morrison knew that his case was weak, so he was willing to appease De Grunne in order to avoid submitting the issue to the courts. Besides, he had accomplished what he had set out to do. De Grunne was happy, for he viewed the letter as a retraction. Though the evangelists only considered it a rectification, the end result was still the exoneration of the officer.

In substance, De Grunne contended that he had acted at the request of the Kete chiefs to remove illegal Luba squatters from their territory. Since he did not know who the unlawful residents were, he had relied on informers. One of them, unfortunately, got carried away and tied nooses around the necks of the alleged intruders he apprehended. As luck would have it, Vass's photograph made it appear as though a *razzia* were being conducted when it was not. In conclusion, he asked Morrison to state whether he agreed with this account.[14]

Morrison replied that "apart from my opinion as to what the consequence of your visit might have been or as to what your intentions were your statement of what actually occurred is, to the best of my knowledge and belief, practically correct." The evangelist found it very difficult to make even a partial admission of guilt so his grudging response was replete with qualifying phrases. While he accepted De Grunne's account as being substantially true, nevertheless, he offered some clarifications. He admitted that De Grunne had violated no laws and had sought no workers for the State or the companies, but, at the same time, he reiterated his opposition to the *chefferie* system because it served to conceal the return of fugitive slaves to bondage. Almost as an afterthought, he expressed his hope that his statement would "satisfactorily remove any ground for misunderstanding of the true situation." [15]

To Morel, he confessed his true feeling that "whatever mistakes might have been made inadvertently in getting the facts of the incident before the public, it is true that I believe thousands of people would have been thrust . . . into slavery, if we missionaries had not bitterly protested at the time." [16] In the long run, he believed that the reputation of one man was far less important than the freedom and lives of many people.

After De Grunne and Morrison had settled their differences, only the issue of Kervyn's guilt divided the mission and the State. And as regards this dispute, Thurstan, who had taken De Grunne's part earlier, concluded there was "no doubt as to M. Kervyn's guilt." Surprisingly, it was De Grunne and Gelders who provided him with the evidence that Kervyn had "committed grossly illegal acts." [17] Thus even Renkin had to concede that contrary to his initial expectations the charges, though exaggerated, were of sufficient validity to justify a judicial determination. In the end, Kervyn was sent home and Coppedge was vindicated, but only as a result of an administrative ruling that Kervyn had been guilty of negligence and not of any criminal act. [18] Still, it was enough to give hope to Morrison that at long last the policy of "judicial persecution" of the missionaries had come to an end.

As the years passed and reforms were slowly introduced, the United States pondered the question of recognizing the Belgian administration. Since the Protestant missions had strongly opposed the step, they were periodically consulted. Thus the American consul sought Morrison's opinions and recommendations. After weighing all of the factors, he submitted a generally favorable report on June 29, 1911. Trade had become more competitive; the people were no longer oppressed; slavery was not as pervasive, and the position of the chiefs had improved.[19] Even the mission was being treated better. Most consular reports generally confirmed the amelioration of conditions and thus the State Department decided quietly to recognize Belgium's administration of the Congo despite some expressions of concern by the mission boards and the humanitarian press.

Though domestic slavery still persisted in the Congo and the State had not dropped its plans to extend the *chefferie* systems, the A.P.C.M. felt less threatened by the Government than it had during the heat of the reform campaign. Nevertheless, the troubles of the mission were not over, for the tension between Catholic and Presbyterian catechists and evangelists had only increased with the passage of time. Finally, as we shall see, the situation became so bad that the American consul had to proceed to the Kasai to try to bring peace to the area.

NOTES

1. Morrison diary, February 16, 1899.
2. Thurstan advised Grey on this matter that the residents of Luebo were mostly scum who placed themselves under the wing of "the somewhat simpleminded missionaries" and not refugees from oppression and seekers after Christ as the evangelists believed. Thurstan to Grey, April 20, 1911, F.O. 403/425.
3. Martin to State Department, December 17, 1907, pp. 8–9, S.D. 192.
4. Hardinge to Grey, February 4, 1909, F.O. 403/409. Like Wilson, Hardinge was sympathetic to Belgium's cause.
5. In his defense, it should be noted that De Grunne admitted "that all is not quite as perfect with the C.K. as one might wish." The Diary of Mellville W. Hilton-Simpson, October 13, 1908, Royal Anthropological Institute, London.
6. E. Torday, *On the Trail of the Bushongo* (London, 1925), p. 174.
7. *Ibid.*, pp. 175–176. Torday was employed by the Free State in 1900 as a Financial Officer. After four years of service, he returned to Europe. However, in February 1905, he went back to the Congo as an agent of the Compagnie du Kasai. Upon completing his three-year tour of service, he took passage to England. He was then employed by the British Museum to complete Frobenius' work in the Kasai and Lac Leopold II regions. He departed for the Congo aboard a C.K. vessel in October 1907. Because he defended the Company and the State when he returned home, Morel and John Harris let him have both barrels.
8. Henri Anet, *En Eclaireur, Voyage d'Etude au Congo Belge* (Brussels, 1913), pp. 265–266.
9. Morrison to the editor of the *London Times* (March 25, 1910), State Department Decimal File, 1910–1929, Cases 355.56–355A.116/234, Box No. 4258. Hereafter cited as S.D. 4258.
10. Morrison to Morel, March 28, 1910, M.P.
11. *Ibid.*
12. Handley to the State Department, April 4, 1910, S.D. 4258.

13. Handley to the State Department, April 25, 1910, S.D. 4258, enclosed vice-consul Thurstan's report to J. P. Armstrong, March 25, 1910.

14. *O.O.C.R.A.*, October 1910, p. 649.

15. *Ibid.*, pp. 649–650.

16. Morrison to Morel, June 18, 1910, M.P.

17. Thurstan to Grey, March 9, 1911, F.O. 403/425. Thurstan noted, however, that bad blood existed between Kervyn and De Grunne and that the men seized by Kervyn, supposedly without orders, had been given State medical examinations and uniforms at Lusambo and placed aboard State steamers in a way that the Government could not have been unaware of. Since both men were of good families, Thurstan expected Renkin was shielding one or the other of them.

18. Hardinge to Grey, February 8, 1911, F.O. 403/425.

19. Morrison to Dye, June 29, 1911, State Department, Decimal File, 1910–1929, Cases 855.00/707–855A.51/5, No. 9236. Hereafter cited as S.D. 9236.

9

Religious Friction in the Kasai

Of all the conflicts of the A.P.C.M., the dispute with the Catholics was probably the most bitter. The conservative Calvinism of the American evangelists and the equally conservative Catholicism of the Belgian missionaries complicated efforts to achieve religious peace in the Kasai. Cooperation was made even more difficult by the language barrier and the disparate traditions of church-state relations. But more than anything else, the Catholic identification with King Leopold alienated the Protestants and caused disharmony. On his part, the king not only distrusted the Protestants but the French Catholic missionaries as well. Thus he implored the Vatican to assign only Belgian nationals to the Congo in an attempt to counter what he considered both French and Anglo-Saxon subversion of the colony.

The experiences and prejudices of the evangelists working in the Kasai had a great deal to do with the religious strife that enflamed the district. Doubtless some of the Southern clerics were affected by the violently anti-Catholic sentiments characteristic of their part of America at the turn of the century. Bedinger was just a little bit more outspoken than most of his colleagues when he charged that Catholicism was suited only for degraded savages, for it confirmed them in their innate preferences for superstition and idolatry.[1] As he saw it, Romanism was a bar to true Christianity, for it substituted the worship of saints for ancestors and the wearing of medals for charms.[2] On the other hand, most Catholic missionaries accepted Cardinal Wiseman's view that Protestant evangelists did not lead consecrated lives, because they devoted too much time to their families and not enough to the service of God.[3]

The pattern of religious friction was probably set as early as December 1886, when State officials greeted Dr. William Richard Summers of the American Methodist Episcopal Church with suspicion and perhaps even hostility when he arrived in Luluabourg to set up a self-supporting station as one link in a chain of similar missions that Bishop Taylor intended to establish across Africa. According to one observer, Summers was coolly received because he had become a naturalized Portuguese citizen and carried the flag of that country when he arrived.[4] While it is possible that the sensitive State officers feared that he might be an intruding wedge challenging Leopold's sovereignty, they were probably just as concerned with keeping out Protestants. Whatever their reasons, they made it uncomfortable for Summers despite the fact that his medical skills were badly needed. In the end, he died alone in Chinyama on May 23, 1888, and no one was sent to replace him. However, both the Presbyterians and the Catholics had their attention drawn to the Kasai by his presence.

Since the State was most anxious that Catholics lay first claim to the Kasai, the Scheutists were encouraged to commence work there. La Congregation du Cour Immaculé de Marie was a relatively new order, having been founded in 1862 at Scheut-les-Bruxelles. While in the beginning it confined its evangelical operations strictly to Mongolia, it agreed, in 1887, to assume the additional burden of the Préfecture apostolique du Haut-Kasai. Because their initial base of operations, Berghe-Ste. Marie, at the confluence of the Congo and Kasai rivers, proved unsatisfactory, they resolved to move to Luluabourg. However, due to illness, unreliable transportation, and other complications, Père Emeri Cambier did not arrive in Luluabourg until November 14, 1891, a full seven months after Lapsley and Sheppard had established their station at Luebo.

Over the course of the years, Morrison and Cambier came to personify their respective missions. Each was an aggressive, domineering, strong-willed personality who did not flinch from argument or shrink from mixing in State affairs. Perhaps their very similarity of character and temperament made it difficult for them to iron out their differences amicably. Then again, the issue of reform exaggerated the antipathy between the missions, for Morrison was convinced that Leopold had "succeeded in allying the Vatican with himself in perpetuating his reign of ruin in the Congo." [5] What disturbed the Presbyterians most was not the fact that the Catholics defended the regime, but that they benefited from their passionate opposition to every sincere effort to relieve oppression.

Nothing could illustrate their divergence more than the fact that at the same time the Presbyterians were locked in bitter battle with the Compagnie du Kasai the Scheutists were so intimately involved with the concern that some of their stations were named after Company directors who were generous benefactors of the society. And in return for the Company transporting their goods to Luebo, the Catholics supplied the firm with porters to relay the Company's barter goods and rubber from Luebo to Tchitadi. What was more incriminating, the Scheutists did not hesitate to maintain the C.K.'s rubber plantation at Bena Makima. No detached observer could therefore place much credit in the Catholics' endorsement of the Company's operations.

Above everything else, the Presbyterians wished to be free to enjoy the rights guaranteed to them by treaty.[6] To be sure, that is one reason why they reacted so angrily when Leopold denied all their applications for station sites following their criticism of his administration. What particularly galled the American evangelists was the realization that the Scheutists were assigned the very locations that they desired most. This was a heavy price to pay for their boldness, for it severely limited the area subject to Protestant influence. Nevertheless, Martin remained confident of ultimate success, for he was certain that the people "love us, while they do not love the Catholics." [7]

Repeated rebuffs, however, finally caused the Presbyterians to despair of relief through traditional channels and induced them to resort to more drastic measures. While Chester appealed for aid to the American Minister in Brussels, Henry Lane Wilson, Morrison approached the American consul in Boma, James A. Smith. What they particularly wanted, or so they said, was for the diplomats to help them to secure a ninety-nine year lease on a small plot of ground near the village of Musesa. But not even such assistance was enough to enable them to acquire the site. In short order, the State informed the evangelists that the location they desired was surrounded by land already allotted to the Scheutists. And, accord-

ing to the Vice-Governor-General (Fuchs), it was the policy of the
State to award a monopoly to the first mission to lay claim to an
area so as to reduce the possibility of religious discord. Because
they were just as anxious to alleviate confusion and avoid conflict,
the Presbyterians agreed to respect such a policy provided that it
was honestly implemented. What they objected to, however, was
the fact that the A.P.C.M. was excluded from Catholic zones while
the Scheutists were left free to commence work practically on the
doorstep of Luebo.

In response to Protestant complaints of unfair treatment,
Fuchs strove to make it perfectly clear that the State was not
"bound directly or indirectly to place lands at the disposal of
missionaries either for free or for a consideration." [8] In like manner, Cuvelier frankly informed the British ambassador to Belgium
"that the sympathy of the Congo Government cannot be extended
to all Protestant missions equally, as the agents of some of them
have adopted in regard to the Chief of State an attitude of opposition, which has assumed a most reprehensible form and method of
expression." [9] In essence, what both men were really saying was
that the State had no intention of rewarding its critics. If the
Presbyterians insisted on calling Leopold a "vicious and avaricious
creature," [10] then they were going to be made to pay a price for
their zeal. Treaty or no, the Belgian monarch had no intention of
strengthening the position of the Protestants in his dominion while
they were unrelenting in their criticism.

By this time, Morrison was most concerned to induce the
United States to intervene in the Congo. In order to bring about
that end, he deliberately selected a site which he knew would be
rejected. As he freely confessed to Smith, his "object in making the
request for a concession was to show you that the Government
would not grant it." [11] What he hoped would happen was that the
consul would feel personally affronted by the rejection and write to
Washington suggesting the need of immediate remedial measures.
As it turned out, that is exactly what happened. Smith's reaction,
in part, may have been due to the fact that he was the son of a
Congregationalist minister. But the determining factor, no doubt,

was Morrison's uncanny ability to get others enthusiastically to embrace his point of view.

Even Wilson, who, like his predecessor, Townsend, had previously been tepid in his support of the reform cause, became quite heated when the State declined to grant the lease at Musesa. In the wake of the refusal, he demanded an immediate clarification of the Government's concession policy. When, after four months, all that he received was a vague reply indicating that no decisions would be rendered on such matters while annexation talks were proceeding,[12] he became so excited and disturbed that one of his superiors in Washington, Second Assistant Secretary of State Alvey A. Adee, concluded that he had lost his sense of perspective.

In seeking Root's support on this issue, Chester took great pains to let the Secretary of State know that his wife, like Root, was a lineal descendant of Major Simon Willard of Concord. As if that were not enough, he noted that one of the diplomat's old friends worked in the foreign mission office of the church in Nashville.[13] No doubt, Chester hoped that the friends and faith that they shared in common would incline Root to protect the mission's interests. Though such considerations probably had little effect on Root's thinking on this issue, nevertheless, he did agree that Leopold had obviously violated certain articles of his treaty with the United States.

On Root's instructions, therefore, Wilson redoubled his efforts to force the agents of the Congo Government to sell or to lease lands to the American missions. In concert with the British Ambassador, he vigorously protested the State's denial of rights guaranteed by treaty to all Protestant evangelists. So that there would be no mistake about it, he made it quite clear that Washington believed that the status of the annexation talks had nothing at all to do with the responsibility of the administration to honor its obligations.[14] In the end, none of this made any impression on Cuvelier, who continued to insist that the Free State had not contested or limited the treaty rights of the Americans in any way.[15]

At the same time in Boma, Smith was equally incensed by the State's handling of the matter. According to him, it was a classic example of "the chicanery and double-dealing which mark nearly every official act of the Kongo's administration." [16] To his way of thinking, it was unmistakable proof of the Government's determination to punish anyone who dared to speak the truth about what was happening. The only way to put an end to such treatment, he concluded, was for Washington to stop turning the other cheek.

In Brussels, meantime, Wilson raised the issue once again with the foreign minister. He specifically informed him that the United States "would be especially pleased to see the right accorded to American Christian missionaries to secure reasonable sized tracts of land . . . in permanent holding, to be used for missionary sites and schools." [17] Since, by that time, annexation was a virtual certainty, the foreign minister's reply was conciliatory. Root was assured that he would "find gratification in the Belgian Government's desire to please a friendly power." [18] As a sign of good faith, the unpopular and inoperative application procedure was abandoned.[19] Even more important, Belgium promised Sir Edward Grey that when it assumed control of the colony, it would provide "facilities to religious missions for the acquisition of land necessary for the prosecution of missionary work." However, it still reserved the right to determine which sites could not be alienated as not being in the best interests of the colony. Moreover, under no circumstances would it make grants to any mission which would not agree to respect the laws and public officials of the Congo.[20]

In an effort to find out whether Belgium had truly changed its attitude, Morrison, on August 30, 1909, applied for a concession of nine hectares near the village of Bena Mpeta. But even with the assistance of De Grunne, it took until January 29, 1912, before the Government gave its assent. Without exaggeration, that January date was a very important occasion for the Presbyterians, for it ended fourteen years of official disapproval. At long last, the American Presbyterian Congo Mission was free to expand anew. With great rejoicing, the post, which was located some 150 miles northeast of Luebo, was named Mutoto, in honor of Mrs. Morrison who had died in 1910.[21]

When the Presbyterians began operations at Mutoto, they found it very difficult to provision the station. Since Lusambo was closer to Mutoto than Luebo and was accessible to steamers all year round, the evangelists sought permission to establish a supply depot there. It was strategically located on the north bank of the Sankuru River approximately 550 miles by water from Luebo and half that distance overland. However, despite the fact that many Protestants resided there as employees of the Company and the State, the Catholics enjoyed a monopoly in the region.[22] The A.P.C.M. application was therefore strongly opposed by the Scheutists. Still it took only seven months for the Government to give its approval, whereas it had taken almost four years to secure Mutoto. The Presbyterians owed their success in this matter almost entirely to the Reverend Henri Anet, a Belgian Protestant, who handled the negotiations.[23]

Though the State acceded to their request, it did so with the understanding that the A.P.C.M. was to refrain from proselytizing in the area. When Dr. S. H. Wilds, who was acting as Legal Representative of the mission, in the absence of Morrison, protested this impediment, Anet informed him that it was the only way that he could overcome Catholic objections to the concession. Wilds, however, was not prepared to accept such an answer, for it appeared to him that the State was treating the Presbyterians shabbily. Therefore, he appealed to the American consul to take whatever steps might be called for to oblige Belgium to honor the Berlin Act and *la Charte Coloniale*.[24]

While on the surface the dispute seemed to be nothing more than a contest to control a town which even Bedinger described as a "cesspool of iniquity," the real issue at stake was whether the inhabitants of each village, if they rejected the Catholics, would be left free to choose their own faith without fear of State reprisal. De Grunne had pledged this to James O. Reavis when the Coordinate Secretary of Foreign Missions of the Presbyterian Church in the United States had visited Luebo in May 1910.[25]

As much as the Protestants resented being circumscribed in their evangelical work, they were even more upset by the threats to their persons and the besmirching of their reputations. The Reverend Charles Crane bitterly complained that the Catholics at Lusambo "bribed the native chiefs . . . to burn down our sheds, and

to kick the people out of the shed while they were at worship."
Moreover, he added that "they spread tales about us that we burn
the hair off the heads of our converts and throw them into the
stream and only those who can swim are taken into the Church." [26]
Père Robert Bracq recalled similar treatment at Luebo where
Protestant catechists went about spreading the story that Catholics
ate children and corpses.[27] More than likely, the neophytes of both
faiths acted on their own initiative in disseminating such propaganda.

In the days after annexation, the alliance forged between the
Belgian socialists and the Presbyterian evangelists during the libel
trial held firm as Vandervelde continued to press the Protestants'
cause and to defend their interests. Though he could not "share
their religious convictions," he wrote to a friend that "from the
standpoint of humanity, my heart is in unison with theirs." [28] Like
them, he was quite critical of the Scheutists. Of course, to some
extent, he was primarily motivated by a desire to hurt the ruling
Catholic party at home, which is why Renkin came to the defense
of the Belgian evangelists. While he conceded that Cambier, who
was a Wallon like Bracq, was a difficult person to get along with,
he wished it generally known that it was partly due to his courage
and patriotism that State authority was so firmly established in the
Kasai.[29] Therefore, he tended to ignore charges that Cambier
illegally brewed a *liquer verte* named for the town of his birth. As
was to be expected, those who enjoyed Scheutist hospitality and
something good to drink paid no attention to the legal prohibi-
tion,[30] leaving the teetotaling Presbyterians to complain through
Vandervelde.

The most serious of all the charges raised against the Scheutists
by the A.P.C.M. or by Vandervelde concerned the "sacerdotal
honor" of Cambier himself. This was a matter of great consequence, for Cambier was a respected and influential church leader.
All of the facts are not clear, but apparently a young Muluba girl
charged that he had committed an impropriety. The accusation
was verified by P. M. Leclercq, who investigated the case for the
State. In turn, his report was substantiated by his superior, Munch
Larsen Naur, who earlier had been such a nuisance to the

A.P.C.M. To make the affair even graver, anti-clerical forces exploited the matter in the Belgian *parlement*.

As a result, Cambier became a martyr in the eyes of the Catholic party in Belgium and demands were made that the Government act to rectify an obvious miscarriage of justice. One of the loudest voices to be heard was that of Cambier himself, who insisted that the local inquiry had been distinguished only for its "légèrité et partialité." Thus he asked the State to exculpate him of any wrongdoing. Bishop Roelens seconded his plea on the ground that the reports of Leclercq and Naur reflected only their anti-clerical and anti-missionary bias. The Vatican also expressed its concern for the fate of a valuable servant of the Church.[31] Though Renkin would have preferred not to have challenged the integrity of the two magistrates, he bowed to great pressure and agreed to reopen the case.

In February 1913, Charles Duchesne was assigned the responsibility of determining what were the true facts of the dispute. On the basis of his findings, he recommended the rejection of the principal "slander" of the young Muluba girl and the removal of the eager young magistrate who had attached so much importance to the charge. Despite his exoneration, or perhaps as the price of it, Cambier left the Congo the following July. Ostensibly, he departed in order to attend to an injury he had sustained three years earlier.[32]

Unfortunately, but not unexpectedly, the affair exacerbated the ill feeling between the Catholics and Presbyterians in the Kasai and led to an unpleasant incident. It occurred when the Reverend Charles Crane encountered an enthusiastic Catholic catechist in June 1913. In line with Scheutist propaganda, the militant convert denounced the itinerating evangelist as an adulterer. The happily married missionary lost his temper and in retaliation charged that Cambier had been discharged for having a mistress and child. Their exchange came to the attention of Père Robert Bracq, who maintained that Crane was guilty of public calumny in that he had sullied Cambier's honor and reputation. But Leclercq disagreed and dismissed the charge. According to the *Missionary Survey,* he did so because the disreputable priest (Cambier?) had indeed been

sent home and forbidden ever to return.[33] There is a good deal of
confusion surrounding the Cambier affair, and much secrecy;
hence it is possible that these sundry accusations involved more
than one cleric.

On one other occasion before his removal, Leclercq proved to
be the *bête noire* of the Catholics. In this instance, the Scheutist
Fathers complained that Motte Martin deliberately confiscated the
brass medals they had distributed to village children. Martin,
however, insisted that he had only received the medals which were
actually taken away from them by the children's Protestant parents. In the end, Leclercq sided with Martin and dismissed the case
for lack of evidence. By this juncture, though, vindication no
longer satisfied the Presbyterians, for they were tired of being
dragged into court over what they considered trifles. Wilds, therefore, implored the American minister to Belgium to see to it that
the Catholics ceased manufacturing difficulties for the A.P.C.M.[34]

When the minister brought this matter to Renkin's attention,
the Colonial Secretary indicated that he was aware of the situation
and doing everything possible in his power to restore religious
harmony. The foreign minister, equally concerned, took the opportunity to discuss the matter with Morrison when the evangelist
passed through Brussels in November 1913. From what Davignon
gathered, the turmoil was probably due, in part, to the inexperience of interim mission leaders, for Morrison supposedly reported
that calm had prevailed when he had left the field just eighteen
months earlier. For a while after their friendly conversation, it
appeared that amity might be assured in the future, but that proved
to be an idle dream.

Conditions had deteriorated to the point where even if both
sides had suddenly decided to submerge their differences, it would
have been impossible to maintain religious peace in the Kasai, for
the missionaries had by now succeeded in imparting their prejudices and distrusts to their African converts. Where once, at least,
there had been religious understanding and harmony, intolerance
and disharmony now divided the people. Unfortunately, the Kasai
—and it was not unique in this respect—was torn by paroxysms of
violence in the name of God because a few narrow-minded men of

both faiths, who honored no teaching but their own, had introduced sectarian hatreds foreign to the Congo. This situation would not have occurred if the evangelists had conceived of the necessity of emphasizing the importance of religious liberty. Since the clerics were incapable, for the most part, of transcending the contemporary religious climate of bitterness and suspicion, their converts not uncommonly demonstrated their fervor by attacking those who were not of their persuasion. In the process of propagating their own distinct creed, each side thought nothing of painting a distorted picture of the other's doctrines. Furthermore, few clerics saw the need to consult in an effort to moderate the strife which their competition engendered. Between the various Protestant denominations, at least, there was a measure of cooperation and some degree of friendship, but no such spirit brought the Presbyterians and the Catholics together in the Kasai in the early decades of the twentieth century.

During the First World War, the situation became even more tense. Most of the A.P.C.M.'s difficulties were not officially inspired, but rather the result of Belgium's weak position in the Congo during the conflict. In a time of defeat at home and growing anti-European sentiment among the Africans, the petty disagreements of the missionaries did not seem very important to the Government. The Presbyterians saw things differently, however, for they viewed the Catholics and not the Germans as their chief enemy. They were so preoccupied with their own local struggle that Edmiston even employed military terminology in his diary to indicate how he was "making war on the Catholics" who tried to settle in Ibaanc.[35] At first, Morrison believed that the mission's troubles stemmed from Belgium's resentment of America's neutrality, but not even the entry of the United States into the war in April 1917 brought relief to the Presbyterians.

If lies and rumors had been the only weapons used by the Catholics, then the Americans would not have been overly concerned. But a number of incidents occurred which led the Presbyterians to conclude that they were the victims of a deliberate campaign of harassment. According to the Reverend Plumer Smith, relations had become so bad that by the early part of 1916

Catholics were beating Protestant converts and tearing down church sheds.[36] Moreover, within the space of just a few months, the Reverends R. D. Bedinger, Motte Martin, W. F. McElroy, George T. McKee, and Dr. Robert D. King were all greeted with abuse and showered with filth in the vicinity of Scheutist stations. In every instance, Smith maintained, a priest was observed passively watching the disturbance.[37] Complaints to the State brought no satisfaction. And much to the dismay of the Presbyterians, they could no longer appeal to their own consul, for he had been withdrawn to London for the duration of the war.

As a last resort, the Presbyterians sought to secure the support of the other Protestant missions whose delegates convened in Luebo for the United Missionary Conference of 1918. At one of the sessions, Bedinger deplored the unwillingness of the Catholics to bring about an improvement in relations. But more than likely, one reason for Catholic coolness was Bedinger's advocacy of a campaign to proselytize Catholic converts. His inability to appreciate that such an effort would only invite disorder and violence demonstrates that both sides were to blame for the turbulence. As it was, most of the incidents occurred when A.P.C.M. workers approached Catholic villages. In the end, the Free Church delegates condemned the climate of violence which threatened the Presbyterians and petitioned the provincial administration to end the subversion of religious liberty in the Kasai.[38] It was Morrison's last triumph, for he died on March 14, 1918.

Motte Martin was in Le Havre seeking a promise of relief from the Belgian Government in Exile when he learned of Morrison's death. With the aid of the American Ambassador, Brand Whitlock, he was able to secure a meeting with Renkin. Martin considered the interview unsatisfactory, for Renkin would assign no one but the Governor-General to investigate his claim that the A.P.C.M. was the target of State-approved Scheutist intimidation. Because his demand for an unbiased commission was rejected, Martin decided to try his luck in Washington. Whitlock tried to persuade him to wait until the war was ended, but Martin was as impatient a man as Morrison. Since he could not dissuade him, Whitlock warned Secretary of State Robert Lansing of his coming and indicated that he was an honest and sincere person who was capable of untold mischief.[39] Like Morrison, Martin let nothing detract him from his single-minded concern for the fate of the mission. That was probably the reason he was able to get the State Department to agree to reopen the consulate at Boma. Furthermore, the Government assured Martin that the consul would undertake a full study of conditions in the Kasai.[40] Washington kept its word, but only after the war had ended.

Reed Paige Clark left Luanda in Portuguese Angola for the Kasai in October 1919 to ascertain the reasons for the religious turmoil there. Clark, who was a New Hampshire Baptist, collaborated very closely with Martin, at whose behest he had been sent. In the course of his inspection tour, he stopped at nine Scheutist stations and four Protestant stations. Though he considered it unnecessary to confer with the Catholics, he did accept their depositions when making courtesy calls. He also interviewed the Christian and Missionary Alliance representative at Boma, the Disciples of Christ worker at Bolenge, as well as several Government officials and agents of the Forminière Company, an important diamond concern in the Kasai. When he had finished, Clark marked his report confidential and submitted it directly to the State Department.[41]

Clark determined that most of the ferment occurred in the vicinity of Bulape (Bakwa N' Zeba) which was located approximately 64 miles north of Luebo and was the main base for A.P.C.M. efforts to evangelize the Kuba. As such, it had become a target for fanatical Catholic converts who violated its precincts three times between July 1917 and January 1919. The most serious incident involved an African girl who spurned the Catholic catechist to whom she was betrothed and sought refuge with her Protestant brother in Bulape in May 1919. To her delight, the head of the station, the Reverend H. Washburn, agreed to grant her sanctuary. But hot on her heels, a Catholic chief forced his way into the mission compound and threatened to destroy it unless the fugitive was given up. In response, Washburn pulled the chief's ears and nose and ordered him to leave.[42] This almost precipitated a small-scale war. Seeing that the situation was almost out of hand,

Père Robert Bracq rushed to the scene together with the Government representative at Mushenge. That officer called for the return of the girl to her intended, but he too was rebuffed. The Protestants would not even consider such a request until the intruders had been dealt with. As a compromise, the girl, Kama, was allowed to stay, and the dowry was returned. In the end, only one man was punished, though he was considered innocent by the Presbyterians.

On the basis of his careful evaluation of all the evidence he had collected, Clark came to the conclusion that: (1) the ambuscades of the Protestant clerics were not spontaneous but had been planned; (2) the assailants, who wore religious medals and shouted anti-Protestant epithets, had clearly come from Catholic stations; and (3) the persons responsible for the incidents were the Scheutist Fathers who had failed to restrain their adherents beforehand or discipline them afterward. As far as the consul was concerned, the weight of evidence was sufficient to ground "a strong presumption of complicity on the part of the Catholic mission" in a campaign to intimidate the Presbyterians.[43]

Naturally, not everything that the Protestants did found favor with Clark. In particular, he criticized their lack of tact in welcoming to their fold Père Joseph Savels. This apostate priest, who had been the Supérier of the Scheutist Mission at Lusambo and one of the most influential Catholics in the Kasai, had become a Lutheran during the war, in London, and had married. Savels' conversion caused a profound sensation in Belgium and much consternation in the Congo. Clark believed that the Presbyterians had demonstrated poor judgment by offering him a place at their mission,[44] as it was an invitation to trouble. Though he conceded that it was a *coup* of sorts, nevertheless, he considered the decision destructive of religious concord.

On the whole, Clark held the Scheutists mainly to blame for the disorders. Compared to the Presbyterians, he thought them poorly educated, narrow-minded, excessively suspicious and intolerant.[45] While he did not contend that the State was responsible for the actual assaults, he did condemn the Government for failing to punish the perpetrators. According to him, religious peace would never be realized until the Government took positive measures to guarantee the rights stipulated in the Berlin Act. Above all, he stressed how vital it was for the people to enjoy the opportunity to select their faith freely without fear of repercussions.[46]

Anyone assessing Clark's report must remember that he was an American Protestant investigating the complaints of American Protestants. His guide and most of his informants were also Protestants. While his findings might not have been overtly dictated by bias, in every questionable case the Presbyterians received the benefit of the doubt. If he erred at all, it was in underestimating the extent to which the Protestants provoked the incidents by penetrating Catholic strongholds. Still, this should not detract from the essential accuracy of his conclusions. Like almost every other observer with some claim to objectivity who investigated the charges of the Southern Presbyterians over the years, he found them based on fact.

Though conditions in the Congo improved after the war, the Americans still experienced some difficulties with the Scheutists. On one occasion during an argument between Bracq and Washburn over which of them was to prevail at Mushenge, tempers became so heated that the Catholic allegedly drew out a gun in the presence of the *Nyimi*. Moreover, in 1927 Catholic and Protestant catechists took to ambushing each other so often in the region south of Bulape that the *Force Publique* had to be called in to restore order.[47] In general, the Catholics were always at an advantage because of their closer relations with the State. They were Belgians in a Belgian colony, and, unlike the Protestants, they had no aversion to accepting aid from the Government. However, despite these handicaps, the Presbyterian mission continued to grow. But while the Luba and Lulua converted in large numbers, the A.P.C.M. still continued to have difficulties with the Kuba.

NOTES

1. Bedinger, *Triumphs,* p. 108.
2. *Ibid.,* pp. 177–178.
3. Fritz Masoin, *Histoire de l'État Indépendant du Congo* (Namur, 1912), II, 373.
4. Henriique Auguste Dias De Carvalho, *Lubuku: A Few Remarks on Mr.*

Latrobe Bateman's Book Entitled The First Ascent of the Kasai (Lisbon, 1889), p. 56.

5. *The Missionary* (April 1908), p. 153.

6. Chester to Wilson, September 15, 1907, S.D. 792. Article IV of the Treaty of Amity, Commerce, and Navigation between the United States and the Congo Free State in February 1892 entitled the citizens of the two countries to enjoy in the territory of the other: "a full and entire liberty of conscience. They shall be protected in the free exercise of their worship; they shall have the right to erect religious edifices and to organise and maintain missions."

7. *Kasai Herald* (April 1916), p. 20. Motte Martin came to the field in May 1903. He was born in Marlin, Texas, and attended Austin College and Union Theological Seminary in Virginia.

8. Fuchs to Smith, December 9, 1907, S.D. 792.

9. *Further Correspondence Respecting the Independent State of the Congo, Cd. 4079* (1908), p. 4, quotes Cuvelier to Hardinge.

10. *Kasai Herald* (February 1904) (Special United States Edition), p. 8.

11. Morrison to Smith, January 8, 1908, S.D. 792. Smith arrived in the Congo in June 1907. The first American consul had received his appointment in June 1906.

12. Cuvelier to Wilson, February 7, 1908, enclosed in Wilson to State Department, February 10, 1908, S.D. 792.

13. Chester to Root, March 3, 1908, S.D. 792. The mutual friend was Annie O. Ottoway from Clinton, New York (Mrs. A. O. Graybill).

14. Senate Miscellaneous Document 147, 61st Cong., 1st Sess., *Affairs in the Kongo,* July 1909, encloses Wilson to Cuvelier, March 16, 1908, p. 89.

15. Cuvelier to Wilson, enclosed in *Conditions in the Independent State of the Kongo, 1906–1908,* Part III (1908), p. 35.

16. Smith to the State Department, March 21, 1908, S.D. 792.

17. Wilson to Davignon, April 7, 1908, *Senate Document 147,* p. 99.

18. *Ibid.,* p. 112. The Belgian reply was handed to the Secretary of State on May 7, 1908.

19. A decree promulgated on June 3, 1906, obliged all those applying for a concession to submit full details about the location. If Belgium then raised no objections, the site would automatically be auctioned off to the highest bidder. The State was to periodically publish a list of available sites, but it never did.

20. Belgian Ambassador to Grey, March 15, 1909, *O.O.C.R.A.,* June 1909, p. 245. The United States was promised similar treatment on June 26, 1909.

21. Bertha Marion Stebbins married Morrison in 1906 and went to the field with him. The name Mutoto was given to her by the Congolese.

22. Cambier initiated work at Hemptinne-St. Benôit, on the right bank of the Lubi River, four leagues from Lusambo, in 1893.

23. Anet belonged to the Église Chrétienne Missionnaire Belge, A Free Church without State ties. The Belgian Synod of Evangelical Churches under the direction of Paul Rochedieu was affiliated with the Belgian Government. Representatives of the A.P.C.M., B.M.S., C.B.M., and A.B.M.U. rejected a proposal that American and British missions should join with Belgium in subsidizing the work of the Belgian Protestants in the Congo. The offer was refused as a devious move to eliminate critical foreign evangelists from the Free State. Anet, not Rochedieu, became the Protestants' official link with the Belgian Government.

24. Wilds to McBride, September 15, 1913, enclosed in McBride to the State Department, October 23, 1913, S.D. 4258. After a while, the Presbyterians gave up their station at Lusambo to the Plymouth Brethren.

25. At the Mobile Assembly of 1904, Morrison and Vass of the A.P.C.M. and Stuart and Moffatt tried to replace Chester because of their dissatisfaction over the delay in replacing the *S. S. Lapsley* and the feeling that Chester had not

effectively stated the case for foreign missions. When Dr. Egbert Smith declined to accept the position, Vass said of Chester: "We will get him next time." In the end, Dr. James O. Reavis was appointed to the post of Coordinate Secretary for Foreign Missions together with Chester, in January 1905. Six years later, Dr. Smith finally agreed to accept that responsibility. Samuel H. Chester, *Memories of Four-Score Years An Autobiography by Samuel Hall Chester, D.D.* (Richmond, 1934), p. 133. This story was also related by J. H. McNeill.

26. The Reverend Charles L. Crane, *In the Heart of the Congo* (Nashville, 1923), p. 18.

27. *Revue Illustrée Des Missions en Chine et au Congo* (February 4, 1912), p. 167.

28. Slade, p. 365, n. 2, quotes Vandervelde to Forfeitt, October 31, 1908.

29. Renkin, *Annales Parlementaires, Sénat, Session de 1911–1912*, p. 118.

30. Vandervelde, *Annales Parlementaires, Chambre des Representants, Session de 1911–1912*, p. 165. The General Act of the Brussels Conference in July 1890 banned alcohol where distilled beverages were not found or their use widespread. This was defined as the area beyond the Inkissi River. In 1898, the decree was amended so that the M'Pozo River became the new boundary.

31. *Biographie Coloniale Belge* (Brussels, 1948–1958), Tome V, pp. 123–124.

32. *Ibid.* Cambier underwent seven operations due to the injury.

33. *Missionary Survey* (May 1914), p. 325.

34. Wilds to American Minister to Brussels, July 7, 1913, S.D. 4258.

35. Edmiston diary, January 16, 1917.

36. Plumer Smith to Executive Committee, July 4, 1916, M.A.

37. Plumer Smith to Executive Committee, August 21, 1916, M.A.

38. Bedinger, *Protestant Missionary Conference Report, 1918*, pp. 147–148.

39. Whitlock to Lansing, March 27, 1918, S.D. 4258.

40. Carr to Martin, May 17, 1918, S.D. 4258.

41. Clark submitted two documents to the State Department on June 22, 1921, and July 7, 1921. State Department Decimal File, 353B.1154AL6/4-353M15/16, Box No. 4232. The Report number is 353i 116/. Hereafter cited as the Clark Report.

42. Edmiston diary, May 5, 1919.

43. Clark Report, pp. 6–7.

44. *Minutes of the Annual Meeting of the American Presbyterian Congo Mission, 1920.* Savels arrived in Luebo in December 1918 and became a full member of the A.P.C.M. in October 1920.

45. Clark Report, p. 11. This was a common view of the Scheutists who were of a rural background and whose education was standard, but not "etiquette-polished." It is worth noting that when the Americans were compared to British missionaries they were found to be "better educated, more liberal in their views, and certainly more polished in every way" though "lacking much in the discipline and respect for authority which their British colleagues seem capable of showing." See Castens to Lamont, January 10, 1913, F.O. 403/443 and Thurstan to Grey, April 20, 1911, F.O. 403/425.

46. *Ibid.*, pp. 20–22.

47. Correspondence from Jan Vansina, December 11, 1967.

10

The Kuba and the Presbyterians

From the moment that they arrived in the Kasai, the Presbyterians courted the proud and insular Bushongo. Though they were anxious to save the souls of the indifferent Kuba and pressed their suit with ardor and determination, there were moments when they grew weary of the effort and turned their attention to other more receptive peoples. But even then, they still dreamed of converting the Kuba, for the regal bearing and obvious talents of those people had deeply impressed the missionaries. Because they cared so profoundly about the fate of the Kuba, they were embittered by their lack of progress and resentful of the competition offered to them by the representatives of Rome. Yet their reward for long years of dedication and concern was almost complete failure. The Kuba, instead of appreciating the Presbyterians' interest in their salvation, were upset by the serious threat they posed to their traditional way of life. On occasion, as when Sheppard was able to find acceptance, there were brief interludes of mutual respect and understanding, but for the most part the Kuba preferred the comfort of their own religious beliefs and sought contentment in splendid isolation.

The mission's initial success, as observed earlier, came when Sheppard was welcomed to Mushenge as a resurrected member of the royal family. But after Kot aMbweeky's death and the accession of Mishaape, the prospects of the A.P.C.M. darkened appreciably. Because the Kuba continued to view him as Bope Mekabe and not just as an ordinary evangelist, Sheppard was placed in a very difficult position. Each succeeding monarch considered him a dangerous rival worthy of elimination. Indeed, one of the first things that Mishaape did upon becoming king was to set about executing and expelling all those associated with his late uncle's reign. Such a development was really not unusual for "the children of a deceased king, his supporters, were hated and persecuted by his successor, his nephew." [1] Because of the customs of matrilineal succession and royal polygamy, it was quite common for the death of a sovereign to usher in a period of turmoil and violence.

One immediate consequence of Mishaape's accession was that Sheppard and his colleagues were declared *persona non grata* and barred from re-entering the kingdom. Having come so close to their goal of establishing a mission, the evangelists were deeply angered and frustrated by Mishaape's coolness. When it became apparent that there was no likelihood of his changing his mind, the missionaries reluctantly reconciled themselves to the setting up of temporary quarters at Ibaanc. At long last, however, Mishaape eventually did summon Sheppard to a meeting outside Mushenge in April 1899. Morrison joined him for this confrontation which took place in a small clearing at the edge of the wood. Mishaape, according to Morrison, appeared to be about sixty years old, tall and rawboned and obviously declining both mentally and physically. He sat upon an exquisitely carved "piece of wood" surrounded by his counselors. And, as they soon learned, he had no intention at all of inviting them to the capital. The only thing that he wanted from the clerics was their aid in expelling the intruders who threatened both his throne and life. His own warriors, without modern firearms, were themselves unable to accomplish that feat. Mishaape hoped that the missionaries would be able to persuade the State to suspend the invasion.

Morrison became quite agitated when he heard this news, for the Government had apparently mounted its "long anticipated expedition without giving [the A.P.C.M.] any warning whatsoever." [2] Nevertheless, he informed Mishaape that he had no one to blame for his plight save himself, for he had disregarded their advice to "put in the feather [i.e., be crowned] & open the roads for all to come & go." [3] In his moment of trial, they assured him that they were not friends of *Bula Matadi* (the State), and they offered to help him on condition that he grant them leave to work in the capital. They even selected a site nearby for an evangelical station, which, however, they really did not anticipate they would be able to occupy until the Kuba had been humbled by defeat. Despite the great danger to his person and his throne,

Mishaape remained stubborn until the end and refused to permit
their presence in his domain. A little more than one year later,
however, he lay dead, the victim of smallpox, and of his capital
nothing remained but a pile of ashes, for it had been put to the
torch by a force of African irregulars (the Zappo Zap?) led by a
white man (Ndoom).

Ironically, while Sheppard was earning the displeasure of the
Free State by his efforts to shield the Kuba against further depredations of this kind, the succeeding Kuba monarchs viewed him
with suspicion. In large measure, this was due to his close identification with Mishaamileeng, one of Kot aMbweeky's sons, to whom
Sheppard had given shelter when he fled the capital to escape the
vengeance of Mishaape. The root of the problem was Sheppard's
inability to comprehend how Kot aPe, who became sovereign in
1902, could believe that Mishaamileeng's bad medicine had been
responsible for the sudden end of his two predecessors, Mbop a
Kyeen and Miko mi Kyeen. But even before him, Mishaape had
evinced great fear of Mishaamileeng. Indeed, the reason why he
had delayed putting the eagle feather in his hair was that he had
not "finished destroying all the medicine which . . . [Mishaami-
leeng] had made & put in the ground." [4]

As Verner related the story, Mishaamileeng had contested the
right of Mbop a Kyeen to rule and had caused such a row that an
appeal had to be made to the Government to arbitrate the matter.
When the State decided in favor of "Bope," the victor chased
Mishaamileeng from Mushenge, and the fugitive sought sanctuary
at Ibaanc. [5] Though the evangelists soon realized that they had
incurred the displeasure of the *Nyimi* by affording Mishaamileeng
protection, nevertheless, they refused to bow to pressure and hand
him over to the king, for that would have meant his death.
Whereas the sovereign's partisans contended that Mishaamileeng
was the leader of a band of malcontents who wished to topple the
legitimate *Lukenga,* the Presbyterians viewed him simply as a
persecuted refugee who had shown some interest in Christianity.
When they made their decision, the missionaries could not have
anticipated the extent to which their humanitarian act would involve them in tribal power politics.

At no time were the Kuba more openly hostile toward the mission than when Kot aPe reigned. A vigorous person of commanding presence, he was considered by most observers outside the A.P.C.M. to be enlightened and moderate. In part, he was favorably looked upon because he sought to have good relations with the Free State in order to gain the opportunity to consolidate his position on the throne. But while he may have departed from tradition by welcoming foreigners to his court, he still had no intention of rejecting the distinctive way of life of his ancestors.

Because the Presbyterians refused to demonstrate their goodwill by acceding to his desire that Mishaamileeng be released in his custody, Kot aPe secretly lodged with the State charges of murder and tax evasion against the fifty-year-old Mukuba prince. Then, on the pretext of restoring peace and order in the kingdom, he invited his rival to the capital. When Mishaamileeng appeared, in good faith, he was roughly seized and delivered to the Government post at Isaka. When they learned of the threat to his safety, Sheppard and Vass rushed to Isaka aboard the steamer *Lapsley* in order to secure his release. They were so anxious to free him that they arrived at the post a full day before he was carried into the stockade on a hammock in great agony, for one of his legs had been broken in the course of his arrest.

In response to the pressure exerted by the evangelists, the local magistrate reluctantly agreed to hear both sides of the case. Kot aPe testified that Mishaamileeng had disposed of the two previous kings by burying black medicine.[6] Thereupon, Sheppard explained that since Mishaamileeng had not left Ibaanc for several years there was no way in which he could have perpetrated the foul deeds which everyone acknowledged took place many miles from his place of refuge. In the eyes of the Kuba, however, he still could have been guilty, for they did not believe that anyone died from natural causes. It was universally held that someone with a grudge or something to gain could bring about the demise of an enemy by transmitting hostile forces. Thus Mishaamileeng's evil thoughts and bad medicine alone would have been enough to accomplish his designs, even if he never came near his victims. Since Western justice could not be satisfied with such an explanation, Mishaami-

leeng, thanks to the aid of the missionaries, was adjudged innocent
and released. Thus Kot aPe still had to worry about the threat
Mishaamileeng posed to his rule.

To aggravate matters further, Sheppard was also considered a
rival and deserving of death by virtue of his supposed identity as a
reincarnated member of the royal family. On at least one occasion
that he knew of, assassins were actually dispatched to murder him
with poison arrows. For some unexplained reason, however, they
departed without making any attempt on his life. Sheppard learned
about this later on when Kot aPe, in a moment of contrition,
invited him to his palace for a secret midnight meeting. To purge
his heart of blackness, he produced a leopard-skin pouch and a
banana leaf which he placed over a fire until it became pliable. Out
of the pouch he withdrew some medicine which he bound up in the
leaf and then entrusted it to a courier to be cast into the Laangdy
River where it would flow downstream in the direction of good
things.[7]

For a time, in late 1903 and early 1904, relations between the
Kuba and the missionaries seemed to be improving. Sheppard was
particularly pleased by the warm reception he received when he
visited Mushenge for four days in October 1903. He was set up in
grand style and allowed to seek out old friends and reminisce
about the good old days during the reign of Kot aMbweeky.
Because he knew the language and tribal ways and was confident
of strong support within the tribe, he even presumed to exhort the
young monarch to release some men who were scheduled to be
executed. When he departed, he had the *Nyimi*'s pledge of friendship. As proof of his good faith, Kot aPe promised to welcome
three native evangelists and to provide a home for them.

A few months later, in January 1904, Sheppard returned to the
capital and this time Motte Martin went with him. They were
gratified by Kot aPe's continued cooperation as evidenced by his
agreement to allow a place of worship to be constructed for the
evangelists. His sudden expressions of friendliness led the missionaries to reassess his character. Whereas they had previously considered him arrogant and conceited, now they found him courteous
and tactful. Indeed, they generously praised the peace and prosper-

ity which prevailed in his realm and considered it ample testimony of his obvious ability and shrewdness.

Actually, Kot aPe deliberately set about refurbishing his image not because he liked the Presbyterians more, but because he was anxious to have their aid in his effort to restore unity to his fragmented kingdom. Neither he nor his subjects had any intention of foresaking tested ways and venerated institutions but in order to win the general support he needed, he dissembled his true feelings. His seemingly enlightened attitude, then, was only a mask, a tactic which he adopted to enable him to soften the destructive impact of Western society. Many of the elders, however, opposed his calculated cultivation of the Europeans and demanded their immediate ouster.

Part of Kot aPe's difficulties derived from the fact that there were no shared rituals or common institutions to unify the Kuba. His person was sacred only to the Bushongo and not to the other members of the federation. While the army was a stabilizing force, it was subject to the command of the reactionary *kolomo* who were openly contemptuous of him and unalterably opposed to his methods and certain of his objectives.[8] Unlike the elders, however, he realized that Kuba power was based on a hollow foundation which had already been dangerously exposed by the Zappo Zap. Because he sensed that the kingdom had become weaker since the arrival of the Europeans, he was anxious to avoid a military confrontation. Yet, in a moment of madness, the Kuba rebelled in November 1904.

The first portents of trouble appeared in September 1904, when groups of Luba rubber collectors, living in Kuba territory, were suddenly assaulted. In response to the hurried call for help by the A.P.C.M. and C.K., Lt. Hubin occupied Ibaanc for a few days at the end of the month. At his suggestion, Althea Brown sought safety at Luebo. But she soon returned to her post when conditions once again appeared to be back to normal. Shortly thereafter, the deceptive calm was shattered once and for all as the Kuba raged through the Kasai seeking to eliminate foreign elements.

In the months before the explosion, final preparations had been completed to develop a substance which the Kuba believed would afford them immunity against the white man's bullets. Unless they could neutralize the Europeans' weapons, they realized that with their bows and arrows they would be no match for the *Force Publique*. Finally, a special medicine (*buanga*) was concocted which was purported to turn bullets into water. Kuete Ngola brought the medicine known as *Toong aToong* from Mushenge to Ibaanc. According to Edmiston, Kuete initiated the attack upon the mission station on November 2, when the local Christians refused to accept the medicine from him.[9] Very much like the Ndebele of Southern Rhodesia who had rebelled earlier and the Maji Maji who rose in Tanzania at about the same time and the *simba* of the 1960's, the Kuba were sadly disillusioned by their continued vulnerability in battle.

Still, before their impotence was clearly exposed, they did enjoy a few minor victories which buoyed their confidence. One of these satisfactory encounters was at Ibaanc where the evangelists and rubber merchants were left to defend themselves without State assistance. Edmiston, Hawkins, and Phipps, together with M. van Obergen of the C.K. and Mishaamileeng, rallied the local Christians and rubber collectors to resist the onslaught, but rumors of the impending arrival of a large enemy force panicked most of the defenders and caused them to desert. The gravity of the situation was clearly revealed by DeYampert who appeared during the second night of the rebellion with the sad tidings that no immediate relief could be expected from the Government. The prospect of having to face the Kuba alone with a few weapons and fewer reliable soldiers was enough to lead the evangelists to conclude that discretion was indeed the better part of valor. With understandable regret, they departed for Luebo and sanctuary on November 4th, after two days of desultory fighting. When Edmiston, Hawkins, and DeYampert returned to Ibaanc the following morning, accompanied by three traders and several hundred Christians, they found that they were too late to save the station. Then, when the Kuba attacked once again, even the debris had to be abandoned. It was a sad troop of Presbyterians who trudged back to Luebo carrying the body of van Obergen, who had died of a heart seizure.

The Kete followed the lead of the Kuba and attempted to destroy the European establishments in Luebo. But when they attacked, they received absolutely no help from the six Kete villages surrounding the mission. As a result, the Presbyterians, with the aid of the *Force Publique* and some Catholics on their way to their own base at Bena Makima, easily beat off the assault. Elsewhere the rebels suffered similar setbacks as their advantage in numbers did not compensate for their lack of modern firearms. The back of the insurrection was broken at Ngel iKook where the Kuba were repulsed by a strong Free State detachment bolstered by Zappo Zap auxiliaries who feasted upon the remains of their defeated enemies.

Though the Kuba uprising was a dismal failure, the defeat of the rebels in battle did not guarantee peace in the Kasai, for Kot aPe had escaped and taken refuge in the Lacwaady marshes. In an effort to bring the monarch to bay, Government troops occupied Mushenge for a while in December 1904. Ultimately, in an effort to save his kingdom, he agreed to come out of hiding and meet with Lt. Hubin. The young officer led a token force to Mushenge for this purpose on February 7, 1905. Because the Kuba did not fear his small contingent, he caught them off guard when he suddenly pointed a revolver at Kot aPe. His subjects did not know what to do, for if they struck at the snake (Hubin) then the calabash (Kot aPe) would be broken. As a result, Hubin's daring act succeeded, and he was able to conduct Kot aPe to Ibaanc where the monarch formally submitted to the State.[10]

The debate over the causes of the insurgency generated almost as much heat as the rebellion itself. While the Presbyterians held the State responsible for the shattering of the peace, a number of authorities, including Emil Torday, Mellville Hilton-Simpson, Jan Vansina, and Samuel Phillips Verner, have ascribed part of the blame to the A.P.C.M. for becoming involved in tribal politics. Again Mishaamileeng figures prominently in the picture. According to Vansina, the mission station at Ibaanc was destroyed because the Presbyterians had sponsored Mishaamileeng's drive for power since they were anxious to see a Christian on the throne and had no idea that he was ineligible to succeed his father.[11] Emil

Torday was of a similar opinion. He thought that the trouble began when a mulatto evangelist, whom he does not identify (perhaps Sheppard or Edmiston), tried to place one of his proteges (Mishaamileeng) in power without respect to the rightful order of succession in a matrilineal society.[12]

Certainly this was part of the story. Even the Presbyterians freely admitted that "Maxamelinga, the old bone of contention, is one of the principal reasons for the attack at Ibanje." As Motte Martin explained it: "Lukenge ordered him killed, and he ran to Ibanje for safety and found it." [13] Nor could the evangelists complain that they had not been warned of the possible consequences of their action, for shortly before the rebellion, Kot aPe had made it quite clear to Hawkins that he intended to have Mishaamileeng killed. "His reason for killing this man was because his father had brought the foreigners into his country, and had been otherwise friendly to them." [14] But obviously other considerations must have influenced the Kuba as well, for Catholic stations, commercial depots, and Government outposts all came under fire during the uprising, which was not directed exclusively against the A.P.C.M.

It should also be noted that it was by no means certain that the Presbyterians were as ignorant about the nature of royal succession as some have imagined. Sheppard, for instance, was aware at least by July 1903 that Kot aPe was only following custom in seeking to eliminate the sons of his predecessors. And even earlier, Morrison had recognized the fact that Mishaape was Kot aMbweeky's nephew and not his son. Furthermore, Sheppard had left the Congo on furlough in March 1904, a full eight months before the upheaval, and did not return until October 1906. Meanwhile, Edmiston did not join the A.P.C.M. until shortly before the rebellion, which was long after Mishaamileeng had been provided with protection. Then again, though Mishaamileeng was closely identified with the mission until his death in 1915, he never made a public profession of faith.

According to Presbyterian accounts, they were simply the innocent victims of a general anti-white uprising which resulted because an overzealous State officer arrested Kot aPe for default of taxes. Ordinarily, the Kuba monarch received tribute from his subjects as an acknowledgment of his sovereignty. As long as every tribe honored its commitments to him, the king had no difficulty in satisfying the monetary demands of the State. But when some of his people, as a sign of opposition to his rule, refused to make their payments, he slid into financial difficulties.

Affairs reached a critical stage in April 1904, when the *chef de zone de Luluabourg* summoned Kot aPe to Luebo to settle his indebtedness to the Government. Because he arrived late, De Cock fined him 100,000 cowrie shells ($75), which he was unable to pay. Thereupon, he was put in jail until such time as his subjects raised the fine. Motte Martin was so appalled by De Cock's reckless action that he urged him to release the sovereign at once in the interest of preserving peace and amicable relations. "To alleviate the situation," the A.P.C.M. made the State "a private offer of the whole amount for which he [was] imprisoned." [15] The Government accepted the offer and released the king, who spent the next fortnight as a guest at the mission station at Ibaanc. If they had hoped to benefit from their action, the evangelists were sorely disappointed, for within seven months their kindness was repaid in the blood and fire of the Kuba rebellion.

If De Cock had truly been interested in collecting taxes, he would have been better advised to have punished the men responsible for the *Lukenga*'s financial embarrassment. But he insisted on making an example of Kot aPe. His myopic tactics, instead of preserving the peace, assured just the opposite and testified to the danger of assigning military men to administrative positions. According to Torday, the people were so upset by the incarceration of their monarch that the elders were able to incite them to rebel in his name. They persuaded the masses that only by evicting all the Europeans could they erase the insult to the tribe. Under these circumstances, Torday asserts, Kot aPe, if he wished to retain his position and power, had no choice but to support the rebellion.[16] As the Hungarian ethnographer portrayed him, he was a tragic figure who was compelled by internal pressures to ignore his own best judgment and to participate in the foolhardy uprising. Torday also blames De Cock, for by arresting the king he had undercut the latter's ability to resist the militant demands of the elders. If the rebellion is viewed, in part, as a conservative repudiation of his policy of *rapprochement* with the Europeans, then Kot aPe's reluctance to bless the movement is understandable.

As soon as the fighting stopped, the recriminations began. It appeared to Mrs. Edmiston that "the State officials [were] trying in every way to put the blame of the revolt upon the missionaries." [17] Because the United States, at that time, did not as yet have a consul in the Congo, the evangelists took their case directly to the State Department. Motte Martin demanded that Washington intervene, for the lives and property of American citizens had been endangered. It was his contention that Kot aPe had been "manifesting a very friendly disposition" toward the A.P.C.M. prior to De Cock's summons, but that due to the "grievous indignities and unnecessary humiliation" inflicted upon him by that officer he underwent a change of heart. Then when the mission was in trouble and help was requested, Martin charged that "Captain De Cock . . . at Luluabourg . . . not only maliciously deserted us, by marching eastward, merely to collect delinquent taxes (money being thus made of more importance than the lives of your citizens and their adherents) but he ordered Mr. Hubin . . . to leave us with all his soldiers, and unite with him on his Eastward expedition." [18]

What probably angered Martin the most was the fact that "after the destruction of our mission property at Ibange, and after the death of many adherents, no restitution, financial or otherwise, was made to us. Indeed they pretended at one time that the BaKuba should furnish the material for our new mission . . . but even that was speedily abandoned." He was equally disturbed because Kot aPe "was reestablished on his throne by an official escort of honor . . . and that no punishment was meted out to him for his rebellion, almost as if they approved of our injuries." [19] Martin was even prepared to believe that De Cock had persuaded Kot aPe to surrender by promising him Mishaamileeng's head in addition to an amnesty.

Though the State conducted an investigation of the insurrection, the Presbyterians complained that the proceedings were farcical. Kot aPe pretended to be penitent and as a sign of his good faith he handed over some ragged slaves whom he claimed had instigated the uprising. In addition, he agreed to the incarceration of two of his nephews until the razed evangelical station was rebuilt. Morrison and Edmiston, who represented the A.P.C.M. at the hearings, were totally dissatisfied, for they feared that the Government's coddling of Kot aPe would encourage future dissidence.

Actually the State had a good reason for restoring the *Nyimi* to power. During the period he was in custody, he was permitted to see key military installations throughout the Congo in the hope that when he was restored he would lecture his people on the futility of continued resistance. As it turned out, he did preach the gospel of peace when he was freed, but only because he needed official support to reassert his position. To gain that assistance, he had no alternative but to promise to satisfy the demands of the Administration and the Compagnie du Kasai. Since the Presbyterians did not sympathize with his plight, they were highly critical of his craven conduct in deferring to his people's exploiters.

At home, meanwhile, in response to Martin's appeal, Secretary of State John Hay ordered Townsend to take up the matter with Free State officials in Brussels. To his surprise, Townsend discovered that the A.P.C.M. had previously complained when De Cock had been transferred out of the Kasai. As a matter of fact, the Government revealed that he had only been returned to his old post at the express wish of the Protestant evangelists when they brought charges against another officer.[20] Because they had hoped to provoke United States involvement in the Congo controversy by demonstrating how American citizens had been victimized by the rebellion, the Presbyterians were sorely disappointed by the tenor of Townsend's report. In a letter to Chester, Martin described the report as "relatively and absolutely untrue,—relatively, because it contains half-truths and insinuations which are the worst form of errors; absolutely, either because the writer coolly perverts the facts or shows himself piteably ignorant of them." [21]

In the years following the revolt, Kot aPe found it expedient to cooperate with the State, but he could never reconcile himself to the mission's presence in his territory. Not even when the evangelists tried to shield his subjects from the evils of the rubber system did he appreciate their efforts on the Kuba's behalf. Perhaps that is the reason why the Presbyterians denounced him as a tool of the exploiters and as his own people's worst enemy. One cause for his continued coolness was his suspicion that the A.P.C.M. was determined to replace him with Mishaamileeng. Another reason for his anger was the refusal of the mission's adherents to pay tribute and to provide recruits. He especially resented the influx of outsiders who occupied tribal lands without the permission of his subordinate chiefs, for land ownership, among the Kuba, was the juridical basis of political authority as recognized by the payment of tribute. Yet the Christian converts squatted on the land without royal approval and without recognizing the prerogatives of indigenous local rulers. On the contrary, they looked to the A.P.C.M. for advice and protection. The Presbyterians' claim to the first loyalty of their proselytes infuriated the *Lukenga*. It was apparent to him that while the evangelists may have in theory preached submission to Caesar, they did not, in practice, advocate respect for his authority.

For almost two decades, Sheppard directed the A.P.C.M.'s efforts to reach the Kuba from the mission station at Ibaanc. In the end, because of his close association with Kot aMbweeky and his son, and his own identity as Bope Mekabe in the eyes of the Kuba, he was unable to realize his design of bringing the gospel to them. Nevertheless, when he retired from the field in April 1910, some twenty years after he had helped to establish the A.P.C.M., he had much to be proud of. Though he did not accomplish all that he had set out to do, he always exhibited calm courage and steadfast resolve in the pursuit of his objectives. That is one reason why he succeeded in reaching Mushenge ahead of all others. It was this same inner fortitude that enabled him to overcome his fear of the Zappo Zap and to enter their camp when they were curing the corpses of the Pyaang. As an evangelist, he lamented his inability to convert the Kuba; but as a man he could be proud of his role in helping to bury the rubber regime in the Kasai.

With Sheppard gone, Edmiston assumed direction of the station at Ibaanc. But relations with the Kuba continued to deteriorate. At one point, the situation appeared so threatening that Morrison and Dr. Thomas Stixrud urgently appealed to the State to ward off what they feared would be a second Kuba rebellion. Upon receipt of their message, M. Cambier immediately rushed to Mushenge in March 1916 to discuss the matter with Kot aPe. Though the *Nyimi* assured everyone that there was no imminent likelihood of an uprising, the evangelists doubted his sincerity. At the very least, Edmiston suspected that Kot aPe was about to instigate a lawsuit concerning:

(1) The trouble with old man Muxamilenge long ago, when the mission [*sic*] that Lukenga had killed Muxamilenge.

(2) Long ago when the mission claimed that Lukenga killed 20 slaves and burned them with someone of the Royal family.

(3) When the last revault [*sic*] was, the mission charged him with it when he had nothing at all to do with the palaver. His people did it.[22]

Actually, Kot aPe placed his finger on the pulse of the problem when he met with Edmiston at a conference arranged by the State. After detailing what he claimed were repeated instances of missionary interference in tribal affairs over the course of the years, he pointedly asked the evangelists if they wanted "the Bakuba to put my eagle fether [*sic*] in your hats if so you can get them. You are like animals in the weeds trying to catch me. Now thats [*sic*] got to stop." [23] At issue was the A.P.C.M.'s pretension to sovereignty over the Christians of Kubaland and the evangelists' apparent unwillingness to respect the authority of the *Lukenga* in his own domain.

When, shortly thereafter, Kot aPe died, in April 1916, he was succeeded by his half-brother, Mbop Mabiinc maMbeky (Bope). Bedinger contends that before he gave up the ghost, Kot aPe advised Bope to abandon the policy of hostility toward foreigners "in so far as it affects the people of the Mission. I am able clearly to see," he went on, "that in all the years they have never done anything to harm us or our people; in my degradation and imprisonment they helped me, when I am gone and you wear the eagle feather, send messages of friendship to the mission." [24] Edmiston, likewise, maintained that before the king expired, he had become reconciled to the mission and had intended to invite the evangelists to work in Mushenge. Upon reflection, however, Kot aPe's sudden *volte face* hardly seems credible, especially in the light of his bitter relations with the A.P.C.M. one month before he died. The words that the faltering monarch was supposed to have uttered sound suspiciously like those that the missionaries would have dearly loved to have placed in his mouth had they been able to do so.

In the early stages of Bope's rule, contacts between the mission and the Kuba were, indeed, more amicable. The monarch even sent the evangelists a number of highly valued Kuba mats as an expression of his friendship. Edmiston reciprocated with a generous gift of much-prized salt. Thereupon, Bope invited Edmiston and another evangelist to confer with him in Mushenge. At the meeting, the *Nyimi* suggested that they bury the past and begin anew. However, he would make no commitment to allow the A.P.C.M. to commence operations in the capital. For their part, the missionaries led the sovereign to understand that if he accepted the palaver of God then his reign would be long and successful, but if he chose to act in a contrary manner then failure would be all that he could expect.

Seemingly, the Presbyterians never apprehended the necessity of addressing indigenous leaders with deference and diplomacy. They alternately made threats and demands and then wondered why the kings reneged on their word. Thus Bope, like his predecessors, soon discovered that he could not suffer the presence of the evangelists. His resentment of their independent attitude led him to view the mission with a jaundiced eye. The cause of mutual understanding was dealt another setback when the Reverend R. F. Cleveland rejected Bope's gift of ivory on July 20, 1916, and threatened the monarch with retaliation if he chose to stay at the State post instead of at the mission when he visited Luebo.

What really angered the missionaries was Bope's order to his subjects to vacate the vicinity of the Presbyterian station at Ibaanc. The Government, however, approved of the step, for it wished to integrate the alien Luba and Lulua into their proper *chefferies*. Edmiston, therefore, incensed both the State and the *Nyimi* when he urged the Christians not to comply with the directive. He believed that he was only doing what the people wanted, for they had implored him to write a "book" to prevent the State from scattering the villages.[25] Bope, meanwhile, was really only concerned with reducing the A.P.C.M.'s influence in his territory. Edmiston did concede that it was important to encourage respect for legally constituted authority, but only when it was not at the expense of the mission and its adherents. As was to be expected, much friction developed over this issue.

Since no progress had been made in converting the Kuba in nearly two decades at Ibaanc, the ad interim committee of the mission decided to delegate this responsibility to the new station that was to be set up closer to Mushenge and called Bulape in memory of Mrs. Rochester. For a while Ibaanc was even closed, but it was reopened late in 1916 in response to the impassioned appeals of Edmiston on behalf of the abandoned Christians. From the time of its establishment, in 1899, Ibaanc had been essentially an Afro-American mission station. But Bulape, under the direction of Hezekiah Washburn, was largely staffed by Caucasians. The spirited competition between Edmiston and Washburn to see which of them would succeed in converting the recalcitrant Kuba was the source of the most serious racial conflict in the mission's history. The coolness between the two men probably dated back to 1913 when the mission was rent by factionalism in the absence of the strong guiding hand of Morrison.[26] To aggravate matters even more, Bope deliberately spoke poorly of Edmiston when he met with Washburn and downgraded Washburn in the presence of Edmiston.

The dispute boiled over when the Kuba overlord complained to Edmiston that one of the Scandinavian evangelists, who was attached to the A.P.C.M. for the duration of the First World War, had, in a conversation with other Europeans, called for his dethronement. To appease the *Lukenga* and improve relations with the Kuba, Edmiston urged the mission to order the Reverend Gunnerius Tollefsen to depart. But instead of heeding his advice, the ad interim committee not only decided to retain the voluble Swede, but as well admonished Edmiston for admitting the cleric's guilt to the sovereign. Tempers flared at the meeting, for the controversy served to ventilate the bad feeling between Edmiston and Washburn. In the end, Edmiston lost his intramission battle with Washburn, for Ibaanc was again ordered to be closed in July 1918. As far as Edmiston was concerned, the action of the mission in transferring him to Luebo in order to establish an agricultural training school was deliberately intended to reduce his influence among the Kuba. Some of his colleagues, he suspected, resented him and refused to work under the direction of a colored man.[27] However, he did not blame all of the white missionaries, only a few.

Ironically, when the A.P.C.M. was finally welcomed to Mushenge, it was not because of its preaching, but rather because of its medical aid during the dysentery and influenza epidemics which followed the First World War. Trouble first began when the soldiers and porters who returned to the Congo from service abroad came down with dysentery. The medicine men, who were perplexed by the ailment, blamed it on the daily crowing of the roosters. But the extermination of the fowl did not bring the plague under control. Bope tried to save his life by seeking refuge elsewhere, but everywhere he went, he carried the scourge with him. Beyond burning down the partitions between the Kuba homes in Mushenge, the State representative was powerless to stem the disease. The situation became so serious that the Queen Mother demanded that Bope summon Washburn to the capital. When he demurred, she ordered the removal of the brass anklet which symbolized his authority. The anklet was sent to Washburn to indicate that he would be given full freedom to deal with the epidemic in any way that he thought best.[28] When he arrived at the capital, the evangelist lost no time in quarantining those who were infected and burning the houses of the deceased.

The moment the epidemic was under control, Bope showed his gratitude by expelling Washburn. However, his timing was very poor, for, in December 1918, Spanish influenza appeared in the Kasai by way of Cape Town. Race and rank had nothing to do with its selection of victims. Edmiston and Washburn were both stricken, as was Bope, in February 1919. Again the *Lukenga* found it necessary to appeal for aid to the A.P.C.M. But this time

Washburn was too weak to respond immediately and by the time he was able to reach the capital, Bope was dead.[29] Washburn did the best he could for the survivors.

The new monarch, Kot Mabiinc maKyeen, was almost totally paralyzed. In his younger days, he had played an active role in the 1904 rebellion, but, as he had grown older and had become incapacitated, he mellowed. The evangelists gave the handicapped *Nyimi* encouragement and a wheelchair. In return, he invited Washburn and Wharton to his coronation, at which they heard him tell his people: "I am the leopard, I hunt alone! Following my own will and judgment, I now pledge you in my authority as king of the BaKuba, to friendship with the Mission! Let them come and build their village at the capital! As the leopard tears his prey, so will I despoil those who refuse my commands." [30]

Though for a long time the A.P.C.M. had been hoping and praying for just such an invitation, when it finally arrived the mission delayed its answer. When he received no response, Kot Mabiinc maKyeen came to Luebo to warn the evangelists that he would withdraw his offer unless a missionary was immediately dispatched to Mushenge. But due to a shortage of men and funds, no one was available for such an assignment. As it was, the mission force was inadequate to meet the needs of converting the more receptive Luba and Lulua. After some thought, the Mission Board decided to send the Edmistons to the Kuba capital when their leaves expired. In the interim, two native evangelists filled in for them. When the Edmistons returned to the field in December 1921, they were dismayed to learn that the Belgian Government had refused to grant the A.P.C.M. permission to establish a permanent station in the capital. Thus, for the next eleven months, they shuttled between Bulape and Mushenge spending no more than a fortnight at a time in the royal village. Before they were reassigned to Bulape in November 1922, they had managed to convert two Kuba princes as well as the princess who had charge of the royal medicines, an important traditional post. Though the king welcomed the Presbyterians to his court, nevertheless, he was upset by their success in converting members of his family.

Whether the Kuba monarchs manifested friendship toward the

mission as had Kot aMbweeky and Kot Mabiinc maKyeen, or hostility as had Mishaape and Kot aPe, the great majority of the people had no desire to be converted. Despite considerable effort over a long period of time, the Presbyterians had to acknowledge that they had been able to reach no more than a few hundred Kuba. Bope, in fact, once told Edmiston that the missions were really very much like rival trading companies whose goods did not entice his subjects.[31] Perhaps the Kuba attitude was best revealed by an incident described by an anonymous visitor to Mushenge in 1923. He observed how a young Kuba prince willingly wore a medal of the Virgin and held a King James Bible while he was being photographed in order to assure warm relations with both the Protestants and Catholics. However, as soon as the picture had been snapped, he wasted little time in putting both objects aside, for he had no desire to become attached to either faith.[32] Thus while the Kuba in 1923 were no longer outwardly hostile, neither were they prepared to "accept Christ." Because they also eschewed Western education and employment, the Kuba ultimately were left in a rapidly changing society with little more than the memories of their glorious past. The Presbyterians, meanwhile, consoled themselves by turning their attention to the tribes that were truly interested in the gospel.

NOTES

1. Jan Vansina, "Recording the oral history of the Bakuba: II. Results," *Journal of African History* (1960, No. 2), p. 269.
2. Morrison diary, April 15, 1899.
3. *Ibid.*, April 21, 1899.
4. *Ibid.*
5. Verner, "Empire Building," p. 72. Initially, the trouble began when Mbop a Mabiinc maMbul died in 1885. He tried to see to the succession of his nephew, Kot aMbweeky, instead of the rightful heir, his brother Miko Mabiinc maMbul. His brother, with the aid of Mishaape, came to power and fought off the challenge of Kot aMbweeky until he died some time before 1892. Apparently, Mishaamileeng and Mishaape then continued the struggle for power after the demise of Kot aMbweeky.
6. Because he was supposed to have buried the umbilical cords of his father's successors in the grave of his father, Mishaamileeng was thought to be responsible for the epidemics that killed Mishaape, Mbop a Kyeen, and Miko mi Kyeen. To save himself, Kot aPe turned to the Zappo Zap to secure a potion to provide protection against Mishaamileeng's medicine and the curse of Kot aMbweeky. Furthermore, the bones of Kot aMbweeky were dug up, and his skull was placed

in a basket belonging to Kot aPe and burned. For more information see: J. Vansina, *Geschiedenis van de Kuba: Van ongeveer 1500 tot 1904* (Tervuren, 1963), pp. 324–329.

7. W. H. Sheppard, "An African's Work for Africa," *Missionary Review of the World* (October 1906), p. 770.

8. E. Torday & T. Joyce, *Notes ethnographiques sur les peuples communement appelés Bakuba ainsi que sur les peuplades apparentées. Les Bushongo* (Brussels, 1910), p. 60.

9. Edmiston diary, June 8, 1917.

10. Verner, "Empire Building," p. 73, and Vansina, *Geschiedenis*, p. 329.

11. Jan Vansina, *Oral Tradition: A Study in Historical Methodology*, tr. by H. M. Wright (London, 1961), p. 139.

12. E. Torday, *Causeries Congolaises* (Brussels, 1925), p. 143.

13. Motte Martin to S. H. Chester, November 5, 1904.

14. *The Missionary* (February 1905), p. 72.

15. Martin to Chester, October 21, 1905, enclosed in Chester to Root, January 21, 1906.

16. Torday, *Notes ethnographiques*, p. 59, and *Causeries Congolaises*, p. 143.

17. *The Missionary* (June 1906), p. 256.

18. Martin Deposition enclosed in Chester to Root, January 29, 1906, S.D. 192, p. 3.

19. *Ibid.*, p. 4.

20. Townsend to State Department, May 3, 1905, enclosed in Chester to Root, January 29, 1906. The officer was Deschamps.

21. Martin to Chester, October 21, 1905.

22. Edmiston diary, March 4, 1916.

23. *Ibid.*, March 8, 1916.

24. Bedinger, *Glorious Living*, p. 272.

25. Edmiston diary, December 1, 1917.

26. *Ibid.*, May 10, 1918. With respect to the difficulties encountered in trying to integrate twelve new members into the mission in the period between December 1912 and the summer of 1913, Coppedge indicated that "it is putting it mildly to say there was wrangling and bad feeling, loose discipline and a degree of inefficiency resulting therefrom, as well as numerous heartaches and disappointments." This was in a letter to Smith, July 7, 1915.

27. *Ibid.*, June 22, 1918. The agricultural school was opened on September 1, 1918, and transferred to Bulape in March 1919.

28. The Queen Mother was the head of the royal clan and thus was considered more sacred than her son. She exercised no control over daily affairs.

29. Julia Lake Kellersberger, *A Life for the Congo: The Story of Althea Brown Edmiston* (New York, 1957), p. 99. The author contends that Bope died in the arms of an A.P.C.M. evangelist crying for Washburn to come.

30. Bedinger, *Glorious Living*, p. 274.

31. Edmiston diary, April 4, 1918. Only salt, copper, and iron were desired.

32. Chalux (pseudonym), *Un An Au Congo Belge* (Brussels, 1925), p. 242.

Conclusion

No meaningful conclusions can be drawn about the early history of the American Presbyterian Congo Mission which fail to take into account the role played by William McCutchan Morrison. When he first arrived in the field in 1897, there was still some question as to whether the mission would be able to survive. But by the time his evangelical career was cut short by death in 1918, the A.P.C.M. had achieved considerable success and his standing among his colleagues was so high that he had been elected to a second term as president of the Protestant Missionary Conference. One knowledgeable observer, the distinguished Dutch Reform Minister, J. Du Plessis, declared that "the American Presbyterian Congo Mission [was] one of the most successful missionary enterprises in Africa." [1] In like manner, the Reverend Thomas Ellis Reeve of the Methodist Episcopal Congo Mission praised the A.P.C.M. as "one of the three great missions of Africa, judged either by the size or quality of the work being done." He further noted that: "The largest Presbyterian church in the world, numerically, is their church at Luebo, in the heart of Africa." [2] Though numbers were only a part of the story, the A.P.C.M. could claim 17,268 converts [3] by 1918. That figure represented 35 percent of all the Protestants in the Congo, although the Presbyterians comprised only 11 percent of the entire Free Church evangelical force. [4] School attendance rates reflected a similar pattern of effectiveness. Indeed, only the Catholics grew at a faster pace.

In retrospect, the selection of Luebo as the initial base of A.P.C.M. operations was a most fortunate choice. It placed the Presbyterians within easy access of the Luba and Lulua who sustained not only the A.P.C.M., but the Scheutists as well. Of course, it was Morrison who made the final decision to concentrate on bringing the gospel to them and who facilitated the matter by his translations of Scripture into Tshiluba. The Presbyterians also benefited, in the beginning, from the absence of competition from other Free Church missions. As it was, the Congolese were sufficiently perplexed when they were confronted by contradictory Presbyterian and Catholic doctrines. Most of them could neither comprehend the reasons for the fissures within Christianity nor the historical basis of these dogmatic differences.

Once the A.P.C.M. was firmly established and the Presbyterians had more to do than they themselves could handle, they encouraged the establishment of Mennonite and Methodist Episcopal missions. Because Morrison was far more interested in Protestant than Presbyterian converts, the Kasai was one of the first districts to be reinforced after Belgium's annexation of the colony. Morrison and his colleagues cordially received the newcomers and helped them to get started. Moreover, they recommended spheres of operation and provided material aid and spiritual guidance.

More than likely, the biennial Missionary Conference was held in Luebo in 1918 partially in recognition of the significant contribution of the A.P.C.M. to the Protestant cause in the Congo. It was then, when Morrison was at the peak of his powers and influence and while surrounded by his fellow evangelists, that he suddenly fell ill and died some twenty-one years after he had first arrived in the Congo. Though only fifty-one years old, his life had been rich and full. His saddened co-religionists expressed their sincere regret at "the loss of one of the foremost missionaries in Africa." Moreover, they declared that "his knowledge of missionary administration, his wide acquaintance with prominent Christian leaders, his long study of African, and especially of Congo affairs, made him a statesman among the missionary leaders of the world." [5] In the United States, Dr. Chester eulogized him as one of "the greatest of modern missionaries in Africa, ranking with Livingstone and Moffat and McKay of Uganda in ability and consecration and in the scope and influence of his work." [6] In the opinion of the Reverend J. W. Allen of the A.P.C.M., Morrison was "what a general is to an army to the whole work in Africa." [7] Perhaps the warmest appreciation of Morrison was recorded by his long-time ally, Morel, who maintained that "no one could look into his straight blue eyes or take stock of his erect and vigorous carriage without an instinctive feeling of confidence." In his view, "no finer man ever set foot in the Congo than William Morrison." [8]

A more complete appraisal of Morrison the man and the missionary must also consider his participation in the reform campaign, as well as the opinions his nonclerical contemporaries had of him. To be sure, Morrison is mainly of interest to African historians because of his activities in the struggle to bring about positive changes in the Free State. His success or failure as an evangelist, while very important to his church and to those he converted, was less significant than his role in the movement to deny King Leopold control of the Congo. Such a conclusion in no way implies that the salvation of a person's soul is of little account. It is mainly a statement of fact concerning the notice that lay historians have taken of him.

At the time of the libel trial, Arthur Conan Doyle, the creator of Sherlock Holmes, contended that "Morrison in the dock makes a finer Statue of Liberty than Bartholdi's in New York harbour." [9] Even his enemies, in a backhanded manner, praised the fiery (*fouguex*) missionary by acknowledging that he was the first and one of the most important informants of the Aborigines Protection Society and the Congo Reform Association. Moreover, he was instrumental in uniting the reform elements in Britain and the United States and promoting cooperation on this issue at the official level.

Because of the part he played in the undermining of King Leopold's position in the Congo, some Belgians still harbor resentment toward Morrison. Thus J. M. Jadot not too long ago denounced him in the *Biographie Colonial Belge* as a leading figure, together with Morel and Casement, in the calumnious campaign against Belgium. Jadot charged that Morrison allowed himself to be blinded to the political opportunism and economic greed of his allies because he was determined to create a state within a state for the Presbyterians in the Kasai.[10] Certainly, selfish considerations concerning such things as mission sites and the like did influence Morrison's course of action, but this does not mean that he was not genuinely appalled by the oppressive weight of the "Leopoldian System" on the Congolese.

Conflict and controversy, as we have seen, were very much a part of the lives of the Presbyterians in the Kasai. In part, the disputes of the A.P.C.M. with the Compagnie du Kasai, the Kuba, the Scheutists, and the State were caused by the temperament and perspective of the American clerics.[11] At least some of the trouble stemmed from the disposition of Morrison and his colleagues to think and act like territorial chiefs, unwilling to brook interference from anyone in the zone of operations they claimed as their own. As a result, they ran into difficulties with both State and tribal leaders over such concerns as conscription, domestic slavery, taxation, and the *chefferie* system. No matter what the issue, the Presbyterians could be trusted not to retreat or to compromise. Thus they made splendid allies for Morel and Fox Bourne and all the others who leagued themselves against Leopold.

Morrison was a resourceful, stubborn, and zealous fighter for what he believed was right. Therefore, if anyone or anything threatened the interests of the mission and its adherents, he was prepared to travel to London, or to Washington, or to Brussels if need be, to gain satisfaction. Since he believed that the policies of Leopold were destructive of the mission's goals and an affront to humanity, he enlisted in the reform crusade. At no time, however, did it occur to him that it might be imperialism that was immoral and not just the policies of the imperial power. If Leopold had treated the people humanely and permitted the mission to function freely, more than likely Morrison never would have criticized the foreign presence in the Congo. It was only when the people were mistreated and the A.P.C.M. was intimidated that he joined in the denunciation of the Free State administration and called for international intervention. Of course, he was not unique in this respect.

Whereas it is possible to show the success of the A.P.C.M. as an evangelical force by the number of catechumens and converts who accepted the gospel, it is far more difficult to demonstrate the effectiveness of the mission in the fight for reform. There is no exact way of telling for certain whether the mission caused remedial changes to be introduced one minute sooner than would have been the case if the Presbyterians had never set foot in the Congo. Yet, it would appear that the outcome of the libel trial did lead to corrective measures in the operations of the Compagnie du Kasai. More broadly, if the reformers are entitled to any of the credit for persuading Britain and the United States to pressure Belgium to annex the Congo and then to insist upon significant reforms before diplomatic recognition would be forthcoming, certainly the A.P.C.M. deserves a share of the plaudits.

Whatever one might think about the merits of the reform cause, there can be no denying that the A.P.C.M. was just as competent a pressure group as it was a Christian mission. In both spheres, whatever was accomplished was largely due to the vision and vigor of Morrison. He was a dynamic leader who proved his skill by taking a mission that was foundering and charting a safe course to a secure harbor. Though he was feared and perhaps despised by the State, he was respected by most Africans. Even the Kuba, who disdained the mission, benefited from his presence, for, as Morel noted, at the time of the libel trial, it was Morrison who stood "between the persecuted Bakuba and their Belgian persecutors." [12]

To the extent that the Presbyterian missionaries adhered to Morrison's advice to "remember first and last that the natives should be treated as kindly and courteously as white people," then the A.P.C.M. is deserving of commendation. It was to Morrison's credit that he admonished his colleagues to "keep in mind that we are their servants and not their masters. Under their black skins they have feelings and sensibilities similar to ours, which ought to be respected. If we laugh at their customs, appearance, or fetishes, we destroy their confidence in us and repel them." [13] In practice, however, it sometimes seemed as though the Presbyterians were mainly concerned with suppressing the true spirit of the people by adopting an overly censorious approach to Congolese society. The danger here was that while the Africans might be introduced to Christianity, Christ himself might still remain a stranger to them. It was very difficult to balance the two approaches of sympathy and censure and on more than one occasion the evangelists inclined toward the side of intolerance and disrespect. But then again, they frequently soared close to the lofty standard proclaimed by Morrison.

NOTES

1. J. Du Plessis, *The Evangelisation of Pagan Africa* (Capetown, 1929), p. 219.

2. Thomas Ellis Reeve, *In Wembo-Nyama's Land* (Nashville, 1921), p. 126.

3. *Missionary Survey* (April 1918), p. 242, quoted from *Annual Report of Expansion* presented by A. C. McKinnon.

4. C. T. Wharton, p. 114.

5. *Congo Mission News* (August 1918), p. 8.

6. Vinson, p. 177.

7. J. W. Allen to Smith, August 23, 1916, M.A.

8. Louis and Stengers, pp. 125–126.

9. A. Conan Doyle, *The Crime of the Congo* (New York, 1909), p. iv. This sentiment was expressed by the author in a circular letter to sixty-eight American papers on August 27, 1909.

10. *Biographie Coloniale Belge* (1955), Tome IV, p. 633.

11. Both Castens and Thurstan concluded that whereas Morrison and his colleagues had every right to feel offended by the Government's defiance of their treaty rights, particularly in the matter of concessions, nevertheless they demonstrated such a lack of tact and were guilty of such incivility toward Belgian officers as to make good relations next to impossible.

12. *O.O.C.R.A.*, April 1909, p. 79.

13. Vinson, p. 136.

Selected Bibliography

I am including in this listing of sources only those works which were the most useful and important in the preparation of this manuscript.

UNPUBLISHED OFFICIAL SOURCES

Great Britain:
  Foreign Office:
    F.O. 10/803/805/806/807/808: Belgium: Congo Free State: Administration, Atrocities, &
    F.O. 367/33/68/115/117/118/119/120/166/167/168/259/261/315: Africa: Belgium and Congo.
    F.O. 403/338/351/374/387/388/400/409/410/418/425/443: *Further Correspondence Respecting The Congo Free State*. F.O. print series without minutes.
United States:
  State Department:
    Numerical File, 1906–1910, Cases 1797/350–1806/79, No. 191.
    Numerical File, 1906–1910, Cases 1806/80–1806/205, No. 192.
    Numerical File, 1906–1910, Cases 1806/461–1806/580, No. 195.
    Numerical File, 1906–1910, Cases 12024–12053/60, No. 792.
    Numerical File, 1906–1910, Cases 12053/61–12074, No. 793.
    Decimal File, 1910–1929, Cases 353B.1154AL6/4–353M.112M 15/16, No. 4232.
    Decimal File, 1910–1929, Cases 355.56–355A.116/234, No. 4258.
    Decimal File, 1910–1929, Cases 855.00/707–855A.51/5, No. 9236.

GOVERNMENT PUBLICATIONS

Belgium:
  Documents Diplomatiques, Cession De L'État Indépendant Du Congo A La Belgique, Suite de la correspondence échangée entre le Gouvernement Belge et les Gouvernements de la Grande-Bretagne et

des États-Unis d'Amerique. Documents relatifs à cette correspondence, 1908–1909.

Great Britain:

1909 [Cd. 4466] *Further Correspondence Respecting the Taxation of Natives and Other Questions in the Congo State* (Thesiger Report).

1911 [Cd. 5860] *Correspondence Respecting the Affairs of the Congo* (Thurstan Report).

United States:

Senate Document 282, 58th Cong., 2nd Sess., *Memorial Concerning Conditions in the Independent State of the Kongo* (Morgan Memorial), April 1904.

Senate Miscellaneous Document 147, 61st Cong., 1st Sess., *Affairs in the Kongo,* July 1909.

MANUSCRIPT COLLECTIONS

Papers relating to the American Presbyterian Congo Mission, in the archives of the Board of World Missions of the Presbyterian Church in the United States, Nashville, Tennessee, and in the Historical Foundation at Montreat, North Carolina. Included in these collections are the diaries of Morrison (1899) and Snyder (1894), application files and missionary correspondence dating from 1914.

The papers of the Aborigines Protection Society and Sir John Harris at Rhodes House, Oxford University.

The diary of the Reverend A. L. Edmiston, in the possession of his wife in Selma, Alabama.

The diaries of Mellville W. Hilton-Simpson at the Royal Anthropological Institute, London.

The papers of E. D. Morel, in the British Library of Political and Economic Science, London.

The papers of John Tyler Morgan, in the Library of Congress, Washington, D. C.

The papers of Elihu Root, in the Library of Congress, Washington, D. C.

The papers of S. P. Verner, in the possession of his daughter, Mrs. W. F. Allston, in Cashiers, North Carolina, and Miami, Florida.

UNPUBLISHED MANUSCRIPTS

Rochester, A. A. "The Story of My Life," 1939. It is in the possession of Mrs. Edna Rochester, Jamaica, West Indies.

Shaloff, Stanley. "The American Presbyterian Congo Mission: A Study in Conflict, 1890–1921." Ph.D. Dissertation, Northwestern University, 1967.

Verner, S. P. "Empire Building in Central Africa," ed. by Ralph Graves, 1907. Part of the Verner collection.

BOOKS

Abbreviations:

A.R.S.C.—Academie royale des sciences coloniales. Classe des sciences morales et politiques. Memoires in 8°. Nouvelle série (succeeds I.R.C.B.).

I.R.C.B.—Institut royal colonial belge. Classe des sciences morales et politiques. Memoires in 8°.

M.R.A.C.—Musée royal de l'Afrique Centrale: Annales. Série in 8°. Sciences humaines (succeeds M.R.C.B.).

M.R.C.B.—Musée royal du Congo belge: Annales. Série in 8°. Sciences humaines linguistique, anthropologie, ethnologie.

Bedinger, R. D. *Triumphs of the Gospel in the Belgian Congo.* Richmond: Presbyterian Committee of Publication, 1920.

Biographie Coloniale Belge. 5 vols. Brussels: I.R.C.B., Van Campenhout, 1948–1958.

Chester, Samuel H. *Behind the Scenes.* Austin: Von Boeckmann-Jones Co., 1928.

———. *Memories of Four-Score Years An Autobiography by Samuel Hall Chester, D.D.* Richmond: Presbyterian Committee of Publication, 1934.

Cookey, S. J. S. *Britain and the Congo Question 1885–1913.* London: Longmans, 1968.

Hilton-Simpson, Mellville W. *Land and Peoples of the Kasai.* London: Constable & Company Limited, 1911.

Johnson, Thomas C. *History of the Southern Presbyterian Church,* in the *American Church History Series.* Vol. XI. New York: Charles Scribner's Sons, 1900.

Kellersberger, Julia Lake. *A Life for the Congo: The Story of Althea Brown Edmiston.* New York: Fleming H. Revell Company, 1957.

Lacourt, V. *A Propos Du Congo.* Brussels: A. Lesigne, 1908.

Lapsley, S. N. *Life and Letters.* Edited by J. W. Lapsley. Richmond: Whittet & Shepperson Printers, 1893.

Louis, W. R., and Stengers, J. *E. D. Morel's History of the Congo Reform Movement.* Oxford: Clarendon Press, 1968.

Sheppard, W. H. *Presbyterian Pioneers in Congo.* Richmond: Presbyterian Committee of Publication, 1917.

Slade, R. M. *English-Speaking Missions in the Congo Independent State, 1878–1908.* Brussels: A.R.S.C., 1959.

Tempels, P. *Bantu Philosophy.* Translated by C. King. Paris: Collection Presence Africaine, 1959.

Torday, E. *Causeries Congolaises.* Brussels: Albert Dewit, 1925.

———. *On the Trail of the Bushongo.* London: Seeley, Service & Co., Limited, 1925.

———, and Joyce, T. *Notes ethnographiques sur les peuples communément appelés Bakuba ainsi que sur les peuplades apparentées. Les Bushongo.* Brussels: M.R.C.B., Vol. 2, fasc. 1, 1910.

Vansina, J. *Geschiedenis van de Kuba: Van ongeveer 1500 tot 1904.* Tervuren: M.R.A.C., No. 42, 1963.

———. *Le Royaume Kuba.* Tervuren: M.R.A.C., No. 49, 1964.

———. "Du royaume kuba au 'territoire des Bakuba,'" *Etudes Congolaises,* XII, No. 2 (April–June 1969), 3–54. [This article appeared too late to be cited in the Notes.]

———. *Les tribus Ba-Kuba et les peuplades apparentées.* London: International African Institute, 1954.

Verner, S. P. *Pioneering in Central Africa.* Richmond: Presbyterian Committee of Publication, 1903.

Vinson, T. C. *William McCutchan Morrison: Twenty Years in Central Africa.* Richmond: Presbyterian Committee of Publication, 1921.

Wharton, C. T. *The Leopard Hunts Alone.* New York: Fleming H. Revell Company, 1927.

Wharton, E. T. *Led in Triumph.* Nashville: Board of World Missions, Presbyterian Church, U. S., 1952.

RELEVANT PERIODICAL PUBLICATIONS

Christian Observer.

Kasai Herald.

The Missionary (name changed to *Missionary Survey*).

Official Organ of the Congo Reform Association.

United Missionary Conferences in the Congo: Report of the Conference of Missionaries Working in Congoland. 1902–1918.

ARTICLES

Adjei, A. "Imperialism and Spiritual Freedom an African View," *The American Journal of Sociology*, L, No. 3 (November 1944), 189–198.

Bedinger, R. D. "Althea Brown Edmiston," in *Glorious Living*, ed. by H. P. Winsborough and S. L. V. Timmons. Atlanta: Committee on Woman's Work in the Presbyterian Church, U. S., 1937.

Louis, W. R. "Roger Casement and the Congo," *Journal of African History*, V, No. 1 (1964), 99–120.

Morrison, W. M. "The Congo Free State Courts," *The Independent*, LV, No. 2870 (December 3, 1903), 2865–2867.

———. "The Kongo Government and Missionary Work," *Missionary Review of the World*, XXVI (October 1903), 764–767.

———. "The Misgovernment of the Congo Free State," *The Independent*, LV, No. 2849 (July 9, 1903), 1604–1608.

———. "Personal Observations of Congo Misgovernment," *The American Monthly Review of Reviews*, XXVIII, No. 1 (July 1903), 38–42.

Sheppard, W. H. "An African Missionary in Africa," *Missionary Review of the World*, XVIII, No. 10 (October 1905), 739–743; Part II in No. 11 (November 1905), 805–816.

———. "An African's Work for Africa," *Missionary Review of the World*, XIX, No. 10 (October 1906), 770–774.

———. "Into the Heart of Africa," *Southern Workman*, XXII (December 1893), 182–187.

———. "Light in Darkest Africa," *Southern Workman* (April 1905), 218–227.

Torday, E. "The Kingdom of Bushongo," *Pulitzer's Magazine*, XXXII, No. 6 (October 1913), 16–19.

———. "Land and Peoples of the Kasai Basin," *The Geographical Journal*, XXXVI, No. 1 (July 1910), 26–57.

Vansina, J. "Les Croyances Religieuses des Kuba," *Zaire*, XII, No. 7 (1958), 725–758.

———. "Les valeurs culturelles des Bushong," *Zaire*, VIII, No. 9 (November 1954), 899–910.

———. "Recording the Oral History of the Bakuba," *Journal of African History*, I (1960), No. 1, 45–54; No. 2, 257–270.

Verner, S. P. "The Affairs of the Congo State," *The Forum*, XXXVI, No. 1 (July–September 1904), 150–159.

————. "Belgian Rule on the Congo," *The World's Work*, XIII, No. 4 (February 1907), 8568–8575.

————. "The Development of Africa," *The Forum*, XXXII, No. 3 (November 1901), 366–382.

————. "The White Man's Zone in Africa," *The World's Work*, VIII, No. 1 (November 1906), 8227–8236.

Index